THE STREETS OF LONDON

THE STREETS OF LONDON

BLUE BIRD
PERFECT
FOOD
AND
NO
MUSIC

PAVILION
MICHAEL JOSEPH

THE STREETS OF
LONDON

Moments in time
from the albums of
Charles White and
London Transport

BENNY GREEN
*Photographs selected
and arranged by
Lawrence Edwards*

*To Dominic F., invaluable consultant on
military history*

First published in Great Britain in 1983
First published in paperback in 1985
by Pavilion Books Limited
196 Shaftesbury Avenue, London WC2H 8JL
in association with Michael Joseph Limited
44 Bedford Square, London WC1B 3DP
Second impression March 1985

Designed by Lawrence Edwards

Green, Benny
    The streets of London.
    1. London – History – 1800 – 1950
    I. Title
    942. 1′083   DA684

ISBN 0–907516–59–9 paperback

ISBN 0–907516–20–3 hardback

Printed and bound in Great Britain by Butler
and Tanner Ltd., Frome and London

Introduction

The small child, flung into the maelstrom of London life, naturally assumes that the town, like everything else in the universe, is in what might be defined as a permanent state of permanence. To his tiny mind, contemplating this unfathomable colossus, London is a finished work of art, a symphony completed, a portrait hung, a maze whose last teasing convolution has been laid out. I remember that when I was three years old, at around the time my formal education began, my mother would take me shopping with her, and that between our home and the local grocer's, just behind Euston Road, there was an empty site whose prohibiting hoardings were bright with posters; through the interstices of the planks a small boy, if he contrived to dawdle, could glimpse a vast hole. Obviously there were changes going on, but I assumed them to be the final finishing touches to the urban edifice, the rectifying of a slight oversight. All the buildings which so clearly belonged in London, all the pavements, all the granite kerbstones, all the cobbled sidestreets and all the macadamed roads, all the railinged houses and all the gurgling gutters, all the bottle-green lamp-posts and all the scarlet pillar boxes, were there, in their preordained positions. Behold, the masterpiece of London was complete, and all the artists and artisans who had contributed to the process could now go home and live in it and enjoy it.

There were, however, a few disturbing fragments of evidence to the contrary. Pictures in books, for example, which showed a London easily recognisable as the friendly enormity just outside my window but somehow differing from it profoundly in spirit. Conceivably then, even immutable London must have had a once-upon-a-time? This was unthinkable, like a parent's infancy or the discovery of a new colour. One afternoon my father, a dedicated Londoner and an empirical scientist of whimsical unorthodoxy, took me for a spree on an open-top London omnibus on a windy day so that I might savour the exhilaration of losing my breath to the elements. We climbed the parabola of the outside staircase, sat on a front seat and, as the bus gathered speed along Euston Road, gasped in the face of the wild west wind, an experience so memorable that not very long afterwards I requested a second trip, at which my father astonished me by saying that there were no more open-top buses in London. He told me that *they* had done away with them, just as *they* had done away with chocolate-coloured buses and buses with difficult devices like 'Thomas Tilling' painted on their flanks; what was more, *they* had scrubbed out the device 'London General' from the red buses and replaced it with 'London Transport'. Was my father serious about this? I could not be certain. I knew him to be an incorrigible joker from the fanciful tales he told me about horse-drawn fire engines, and days when steam from train funnels used to come swirling through the open roof of Great Portland Street Station. Could it be possible then, that London was not so immutable after all? Gamely I struggled to incorporate these worrying contradictions into my grand central scheme of urban timelessness.

Although I could not have known it then, I was living through one of the most profound transitions in all history, the grinding modulation from the horse to the machine. As late as the 1930s there were still more horses than cars on the London streets. It was a moment when the two modes co-existed, two epochs whose intermingling was epitomised by that symbolic scenic effect of my childhood, horse-dung from the brewer's dray or the coal cart or the milk van squashed flat into the cobblestones by a passing motor car, and later to be scraped clanguorously away by the street cleaner's encrusted shovel. It was as though history was poised in contemplation of the problem of Dobbin or Juggernaut before casting its vote for the machine and condemning the town to hideous despoliation. I knew that there must once have been many more horses on the streets, otherwise why all those funny little back alleys which had clearly been designed as stables, and were now so carelessly converted into garages or store rooms or dwellings for acquaintances of mine? And why that drinking trough just round the corner from where we lived? That trough remained there for twenty years after the last weary carthorse slaked its thirst in its waters; one day I returned home from a long provincial tour with some forgotten dance band to find that the trough had been swept away in the frenzied preparations for a realignment of the roads around Great Portland Street Station. I had missed the turning point.

If there was a specific moment when the urban horse bolted, then it was 1851, when for the first time in history the townees in Britain outnumbered their country cousins. Perhaps the analogy of the bolting horse is especially appropriate, because from that moment when the British became predominantly urban, London was doomed to the role of a horse-and-cart town struggling to accommodate what printers, with their blind instinct for the Freudian slip, have sometimes defined as the infernal combustion engine. First the railway and then the motor car slashed the town to ribbons, riding roughshod over the most hallowed ground, obliterating venerable landmarks, smashing a swathe through the purlieus of history, destroying tradition and rearranging the prevailing topography with no more concern than a giant swatting a fly. The very dead in their coffins were obliged to move aside and make way for the new age, as a certain architect's assistant was interested to discover for himself in 1867, when the new-fangled Midland Railway was cutting its way into its grand new terminus at St Pancras. Across the path of the Iron Horse lay its last impediment, the crowded cemetery of old St Pancras. The levelling proceeded and scandal erupted when a passer-by insisted he had seen an open coffin through whose splintered timbers there floated a tress of bright hair. The architect's assistant was sent along to see that the disturbed corpses were removed and reburied with due reverence. Later, the young assistant, whose name was Thomas Hardy, wrote a poem about it:

O Passenger, pray list and catch
Our sighs and piteous groans,
Half stifled in this jumbled patch
of wrenched memorial stones.

We late-lamented, resting here,
Are mixed to human jam,
And each to each exclaims in fear,
'I know not which I am!'

A generation later, by which time Mr Sherlock Holmes was attending to the more pressing forensic affairs of the metropolis, the population had swollen to over five million, and even Holmes, that walking A-to-Z Street Guide, must have been hard put to keep abreast of the building of new

streets, new roads, new thoroughfares, new districts. By 1930 the population had reached eight million and was still rising, although it soon afterwards reached its peak and then began to fall away, as the central districts were rendered uninhabitable, first by German bombing and then by the far more terrible destructive fury of municipal incompetence and architectural barbarism. By then the problems confronting the administrators of London had acquired an enormity so frightful that no individual gesture could hope to contain it. The New Age demanded more dwellings, more factories, bigger docks to deliver food, wider roads to distribute it, and still wider roads to placate the motor-car industry. Everything small was under notice to quit: small shops, small schools, small hospitals, even small boroughs. As a metropolitan wit wryly observed, man is born free, and everywhere he is in chain stores.

The effect of this headlong flight into an uncharted future has been to render recent metropolitan history as remote as smalltalk of the Pharaohs. Refer to horse troughs and the muffin man's bell, to wireless accumulators and Clapton Orient Football Club, to tram tickets and 'Stop Me and Buy One', to blue serge and watch-chains, to the Carlton Hotel and Classified Editions, and a man is condemned instantaneously to the limbo of lost causes; those memoirs which are, comparatively speaking, of a very recent, almost contemporary vintage, acquire the patina of antiquity. There is the casual remark of the artist Ernest Shepard recalling his childhood in a house a few minutes walk from Baker Street:

Before the Great Central Line and Marylebone Station were built, one could walk straight across from Kent Terrace, up Alpha Place, past Boscobel Place, and, crossing Lisson Grove and Edgware Road, come to Westbourne Grove.

It was Shepard, portraitist of Mr Toad and Winnie the Pooh, who bequeathed to a mystified posterity the most graphic account of a journey on a Victorian omnibus. The occasion is Queen Victoria's Golden Jubilee; the Shepard children are being taken to see the decorations:

We boarded an 'Atlas' bus at the corner of the Terrace. Cyril and I were allowed to climb up the steep steps, helped by the conductor, and were then handed along by the passengers, who sat back to back on the long middle seat. There was no railing to prevent one from falling off, only a low board, so we clung tightly as we were handed forward. I was first, and in consequence secured a place on the box-seat beside the driver, where a man made room for me and fixed the tarpaulin apron.

It was fun sitting beside the driver. The horses seemed to know of their own accord when to stop, though there were no regular stopping places, the bus halting where anyone might choose. The conductor stood on a little step at the back, by the door. He gave the signal to start, by slapping the side of the bus with the strap by which he held on. Directly the horses heard the strap, and the driver released the foot-brake, they strained forward and broke into a slow trot. The buses were painted different colours, green, red, blue or yellow according to the route, and had names like old stage-coaches. The 'Atlas' which ran up to the 'Eyre Arms' from the West End was light green and the express 'City Atlas' was dark green. The 'City Atlas' ran in the mornings and could be watched from the breakfast-room windows bucketing past Kent Terrace, drawn by three horses at a fine gallop; the top was always filled with top-hatted men with fluttering newspapers. A woman was never seen on top of a bus, the climb up was too steep for the long skirts worn at the time, although a young friend of Mother's called Poppy once clambered up to the consternation and horror of the inside passengers.

One of Shepard's contemporaries, Sir Compton Mackenzie, took a more general view of London bus travel, recalling that it was very much a question of allegiances, and that at his prep school, 'The chief excitement we felt about omni-buses was whether they belonged to the London General Omnibus Company or to the London Road Car Company.' The colours of the various companies were a clear indication of geographical lines of demarcation:

Once upon a time the colours of the omnibuses achieved the same kind of significance that a national flag possesses. Suddenly to see a red Hammersmith bus in the far east of London was like a sight of the Red Ensign in an oriental harbour. To us, familiar with the south side of Kensington Gardens, people who lived in Bayswater and rode in green omnibuses seemed as far away as Ireland, while the white-bused residents of Putney had a kind of polar remoteness.

The eventual disappearance of these rival companies, the institution of timetables and regular stops, the standardisation of London's public transport, no doubt brought with it an order which eased the problems of travel for the Londoner, but sentimentalists like Mackenzie were never in two minds about the vanished pleasures of picturesque horsedrawn confusion:

There must have been many omnibuses of every colour imaginable that I never saw in my youth, and it is a pity that no record of them exists. We took them for granted, and then they vanished like autumn leaves. I wish the colours of those old omnibuses could be preserved by some topographer of London. A book should have been written about them before the motor buses drove them from the scene.

The Victorian Londoner of Mackenzie's boyhood by no means had all the worst of it. When Holmes was sending and receiving all those cryptic epistolary communications, there were eight to ten · postal deliveries in London every *day*. The Londoner had at his disposal more theatres, more bus companies, no diesel fumes, and, a point often forgotten, many more newspapers and magazines to read. In a letter written in 1949, P. G. Wodehouse, wondering how the modern short story writer contrives to stay alive, reminds his correspondent that:

When you and I were breaking in, we might get turned down by the *Strand* and *Pearson's*, but there was always the hope of landing with *Nash's*, *The Storyteller*, the *London*, the *Royal*, the *Red*, the *Yellow*, *Cassell's*, the *New*, the *Novel*, the *Grand*, *Pall Mall* and the *Windsor*, not to mention *Blackwood*, *Cornhill*, and *Chamber's*. I note that in July 1901 I sold a story to something called the *Universal and Ludgate Magazine* and got a guinea for it.

Like most best-selling authors of the period, Wodehouse saw the designers of his books bestowing upon them the imprimatur of the London omnibus; *Big Money*, first published in 1920, had a jacket design showing the occupants of an open-top bus staring down at a passing sports car, a scene which announced the locale of the novel as effectively as if Wodehouse had entitled it 'London, the Story of a Great City'. This tendency to evoke a sense of place by displaying the common or garden London bus was most strikingly demonstrated in 1974 when the publishing house of John Murray issued new editions of the Holmes books, of which two, *The Memoirs* and *The Return*, had cover designs which capitalised on the evocative power of the old horse-drawn buses; indeed, if the hansom cab was the gondola of London, then the bus was its galleon, which flew devices proclaiming not its nationality but the primacy of Nestle's Milk, Pear's Soap and Fry's Cocoa.

So far as the average passenger was concerned, the London bus appeared on its appointed route as though by some obscure process of predestination. A new suburb might burgeon, a fresh community might spring up, a new battalion of commuters might be recruited, and one day, as if by divine intervention, there came rolling along the road that most potent of all metropolitan symbols, the London omnibus.

The Londoner was only very vaguely aware that behind the fortuitous regularity of the London omnibus's habits, there was some kind of vague bureaucratic conspiracy dedicated to the task of maintaining lines of communication, linking the hundred villages, the thousand tribal enclaves which made up London. But it occurred to almost nobody outside the conspiracy that the traveller was being watched over, his desires monitored, his welfare studied with a solicitude which the asperities of a later age have rendered sadly quaint.

Now whenever it became apparent to the executives of London Transport that nothing short of a new bus route would meet the requirements of some newly flourishing corner of the town, or the growing tendency of its inhabitants to move regularly from one specific spot to another, meetings were convened, discussions mounted, debates entered upon, to determine the route and the frequency of the new service. Advance scouts were sent out to examine the lie of the land, and it became the practice of the authorities, once the proposed route had been settled upon, to send out a second group of investigators, a team of photographic outriders who would cover the ground so thoroughly that the drivers pioneering the new route could become familiar with its contours without leaving the garage. The original purpose of this procedure, to familiarise everyone with the nature of the new route, was certainly fulfilled, but it had another function, undreamed of at the time, but now of priceless importance to posterity, to the historian of London, to those who still need to be convinced that change is not the same thing as improvement, to bureaucrats who still have trouble understanding such clichés as the quality of life and environmental pollution. For the photographs of the new routes comprise a unique record of London's external appearance in the period when urban life was adjusting to the onrush of the twentieth century. What was meant to happen to the photographs once their technical usefulness was ended, nobody is clear, but it seems likely that in the normal way of

things, they would have been filed in triplicate and eventually destroyed as their resemblance to reality gradually melted away. Only by a fluke were they saved from that oblivion which has blotted out to so great an extent our view of the childhood and adolescence of modern London.

At some time during the Edwardian era there came to work in the administrative offices of London Transport a man called Charles White. White was a Londoner born and ill-bred who had grasped very early in life the simple proposition that great cities take on the physical aspect they do for a multiplicity of reasons not altogether connected either with altruism or aesthetics. This awareness appears to have transformed White into a cynic of some bitterness, but a cynic not entirely devoid of hope, a last-ditch curmudgeon, whose obstinate insistence that conditions might be better than they were, at last rendered him insufferable to those fellow-workers obliged to come to terms with him. It should be understood that in the hierarchical sense, White possessed no power at all. He remained at a lowly status; executive office not only never promised to come his way, but appears to have interested him not in the slightest. And yet he possessed an authority rendering him immune from the rebukes of his superiors, who, perceiving a certain glint in his eye, took due note of the fervour with which he rode his hobbyhorses, saw that such passion when harnessed to the job he was being paid to do constituted an invaluable asset, and gave him just enough latitude to ensure that the status quo would not be disturbed. In other words, White was graciously permitted to grow old in the service of the Board of London Transport and was happy to do so. The type is familiar enough; fortunately for the English, men like White recur at regular intervals, asserting the authority of their own temperament over more worldly but less fiercely committed colleagues in positions of higher authority.

Very little else is known of White, or about the terms of his engagement by London Transport, and the bare facts give no faint indication of the source of his passion. He was born in Panton Street, just behind the Haymarket, on 11 February, 1876, the son of a surgeon at St George's Hospital who had married for a second time late in life and was sixty years old when Charles arrived. He was sent to be educated at Epsom College, but if White senior hoped that the boy would follow him into professional life, he must have been sadly disappointed, not to say bewildered. For young Charlie seems never to have shown an abiding interest in anything except public transport as it affected the life of London. His first job was with

London United Tramways, where he must have performed with spectacular diligence, for he was later sent to Cork with the onerous responsibility of interviewing staff applicants for the city's new tram system. While there he married an Irish girl and subsequently brought her back with him to London, where he was employed in the Publicity Office of London Transport. It was White who was responsible for the range of the Board's Country Walk books and for the various London Guides which appeared from time to time; in the inter-war years, whenever a new publicity leaflet was issued, it was White's hand that was usually behind it. His precise position and the range of his duties appear to have been so imprecise that today there is nobody able to define them; inquiries half a century later at London Transport prompted the response that 'It is rather difficult to find anyone today who knows much about his work at London Transport, in particular how he came to compile the albums.'

We will return to those albums in a moment, but first it is revealing to make some attempt to take White's measure, if only to discover what nature of a man it was who so perversely took upon himself duties and responsibilities which were clearly not his to assume. Perhaps his colleagues thought he was half-crazy. Perhaps he was. Certainly he inspired little affection among them, and bestowed none. His indefinably privileged position meant that he had the ear of the most exalted figures. For instance, he often performed small tasks for Frank Pick, the distinguished vice-chairman of the London Passenger Transport Board. And yet after Pick died and White was invited to compile the official biography, his reply was that as he had always detested Pick in life, he failed to see why he should erect a monument to him now that he was dead. This admirable integrity seems, however, to have been qualified, for it did not prevent White, when sufficiently roused, from soaring over the heads of his immediate superiors and delivering to the very summit of the Board complaints about his fellow-workers, who responded to this thoughtful frankness on White's part by stigmatising him as, 'An irritable, pedantic man whose pontifications on the minutiae of London sights and buildings was made more infuriating to his listeners by the fact that he was more than often correct.' They accused him of being an obsessive worker, a tyrant, a stickler for the tiniest syntactical nicety, and no respecter of any reputation but his own.

We know little else of relevance about him, except that he was one of those men who write tirelessly to the editors of newspapers, and that he contributed to Trade Union journals of the inter-war years. He enjoyed collecting Toby jugs, and had acquired from somewhere an eye for paintings which encouraged him to give advice on the subject to senior members of the Board. After his retirement at the age of sixty he began working on a series of London Borough Guides for a publishing house based in Cheltenham, and the researcher pursuing White down the corridors of the recent past might be forgiven for assuming that this late connection would provide him with fresh insights, or at least the same insights from a different vantage point. In fact, as a repository for recollections of White, Cheltenham turns out to be even more barren than London Transport. For the publishers of those Borough Guides were bemused to discover that they were destined never to come face to face with White at all. His manuscripts would arrive by post on the appointed date, impeccable in their correctitude; if any editorial amendments were attempted, White swiftly unamended them without consideration for any sensibilities other than his own. But never once did he travel to Cheltenham to confront his persecutors, and never once did they venture into London to confront theirs. In March 1960 the *Brentford and Chiswick Times* reported that this now ancient perfectionist was completing a walking survey of Westminster in preparation for a new guidebook. He died in 1968 at the age of ninety-one, by now a recognised authority on London who received countless postal inquiries on the subject. So far as is known from his family, he remained active to the end.

Had this been the sum total of his achievement, White would be forgotten today, one of a vast army of unsung heroes who perform modest tasks in modest style. But it was not the sum total. During his years at London Transport he displayed one stroke of imagination which ensures his reputation. It concerns those photographs, those thousands of scenes shot for the strictly functional purpose of familiarising drivers with the intricacies of new routes. White, the dedicated local historian, saw instantly that those photographs served a more profound cause, if only by pure accident. They charted the minute changes on the face of London. Without asking anyone's permission, or even informing any responsible person what he was doing, White began to collate the photographs, grouping them under geographical headings, annotating them in an exhaustive, caustic, and at times, comic style. The modern reader need only glance at a few of White's annotations to appreciate what must have happened. This strange character, chafing under the restraints of a philistine world, had stumbled, by pure fluke, on a task commensurate with his grand passion for London, for thoroughness, for accuracy, for the whimsicalities and ironies of time. The fervour comes through with every word. The extraordinary grasp of metropolitan arcana is proudly displayed at every opportunity, and where no opportunity presents itself, then White blithely invents one.

What we are witnessing is an exhibition by an expert, proud to disclose his expertise, and scornful of the quibble that in the strict sense of terms of hire, he has no authority to be performing his task at all. Indeed, long after White had vanished from the scene and London Transport belatedly came to terms with his inheritance, their bewilderment was not the least entertaining aspect of the charade. Who was White? Who told him to compile the albums? Why was there no official record of the existence of the albums? And if nobody had instructed him, how had he managed to find the time and the presumption to lay hands on the Board's property? Had he performed his prodigious labours at the office or at home? (The answer to this question is doubly impossible to find because, by the nature of his official duties, reconnoitring London in preparation for the compilation of a new guide, White had comparative freedom of movement, so that at any given moment, nobody at London Transport knew where he might be or what he was doing there.) And so it would seem that White, who all his life shunned publicity, succeeded in his plan to shroud his nature from the world, compiling his *magnum opus* with such sustained clandestine cunning that its very existence was not suspected until long after his death. We might be forgiven for assuming that no man ever concealed his own tracks more thoroughly, obscuring his outline from the world so well that today we cannot begin to guess what he might have looked like, sounded like, or thought about whenever circumstances obliged him for a brief unhappy moment to dismount from his hobbyhorse. But the irony is that in creating his secret epitaph White disclosed his own nature with far more candour than most men ever do, for the revelatory nature of his annotations sometimes discloses more of the writer than it does of his subject. This is what White has to say of one of the most symbolic of all metropolitan spectacles:

It is a peculiarity of the English in matters of art to accept the most commonplace objects in the way of monuments as a matter of course and to wax deprecative of work of real artistic merit marking a departure from the conventional and the stereotyped. Thus it is with Alfred Gilbert's fountain at Piccadilly Circus.

It is original; it is daring; it is bold; the Eros that surmounts it has life in every line, and the critics who tolerate with complacency the street monuments that might have been designed by children playing with shilling boxes of bricks perceive nought to arouse admiration in the most striking and artistic fountain in London. But Gilbert was mad – and a genius; his critics are sane – and are fools. To the foreign visitor, particularly the Japanese, the Piccadilly Fountain is among the very few street monuments in London that are really worthy of notice. And of all peoples it is the Japanese that excel in bronze. Maybe this is why the Japanese can appreciate what the Englishman decries?

A picture of comical incongruity begins to form, of a London Transport clerk discussing issues of the most abstruse Whisterian significance with Japanese tourists when he ought to be back at his desk pondering the cosmic implications of a new design for bus conductors' peaked caps, of a nobody whose diary is crammed with evidence, not of his own crassness but of the crassness of everyone else, of a defiant autodidact railing at the bar of history against the tyranny of fashion. But most revealing of all, it is quite clear from the theme of that annotation that when something happens to take White's fancy which is not remotely connected with London Transport, he tickles the flanks of his hobbyhorse and lets London Transport look after itself. By no stretch of the imagination, not even White's, could the aesthetic grandeur of the Piccadilly fountain be said to affect the stream of traffic drifting past it. No doubt in his own defence White would have offered Japanese tourists as an example of those omnibus travellers deeply moved by the beauty of the fountain as they raced along it. Whether Frank Pick and his legions would have accepted this as a valid argument is yet another question pertaining to White which posterity finds itself unable to answer. It may all have been unethical of White the London Transport employee, but it was positively heroic so far as White the citizen of a great capital city was concerned. His gaze is wideranging and utterly merciless:

Next year, 1924, the grass plots skirting Park Lane will put forth a wondrous display of spring blooms, the *Evening News* having recently presented 100,000 bulbs to the Office of Works for planting here. It is difficult to keep Carmelite House off the grass, but this intrusion will do something to make up for the disfiguring *Daily Mail* signs set up in various other parts of London.

From which acidulous contempt we are able to deduce that White, the writer of Trade Union polemic, was hardly well disposed towards the social role of Lord Rothermere. As for London Transport, it too must learn to accept the fact that there is no appeal against White's verdicts, and that some of its defeated rivals might have possessed virtues sadly missing from modern streets:

> Old Southwark Bridge was never used to any great extent by vehicular traffic, although it connected Thames Street directly with the Surrey side. The approach from the Thames Street side, however, was by way of a somewhat stiff gradient, which deterred drivers of heavy vehicles from essaying the crossing. Tillings used to work a service of four-horse buses over this bridge in the mornings and evenings. These plied between the City and Peckham and had their regular passengers, among them being Sir Edward Clarke. The passengers knew the driver, and the driver knew the passengers, and the passengers, of course, knew one another, and this four-horse bus of Tillings was a very select affair in its way. It had quite a touch of the old coaching days about it as it came rattling over the bridge with its spanking team into the City.

The obsequious inclusion among the passengers of Sir Edward Clarke reveals White as a man who can see that it was more honourable to have defended Oscar Wilde in court than to have pilloried him in the penny press; at any rate, poor old Lord Rothermere comes in for another savage battering, this time on the issue of the malign effect of the royal parks on the flow of London's traffic:

> Some of the suggestions put forward for 'improvement' would seem to emanate from people who have been in Bedlam but never in Hyde Park. The originator of the *Daily Mail* boulevards project, and those who supported this silly idea may be numbered among them.

White, however, is so prolific with his brickbats as never to confine them to men of one political kidney. In annotating an obscure item of metropolitan history, he is suddenly consumed by an uncontrollable passion to lash out at a long-forgotten political placeman who once incurred his contempt:

> The garden at Montagu House became famous in later years through the gross misrepresen-

tations made up by Mr Ure, MP (now Lord Strathclyde) when seeking political advancement by a perfervid support of Lloyd Georgian land taxes.

White's true political affiliations begin to drift into clearer focus with his discussion of the great Millbank improvement scheme, which gives him the chance to take a swipe at the Mother of Parliaments:

> At the northern end, close to Abingdon Street, stood a Salvation Army shelter, unnecessarily labelled as such, for it could be mistaken for nothing else. Here at various periods of the day queues of ragged, miserable-looking men – the sediment of London's millions – lined up to receive food. As one approached from the southern end the Victoria Tower was seen rising above the shelter, and the spectacle of the Submerged Tenth awaiting their dole of food, within the shadow of the Houses of Parliament, was one such as could have been seen in no other capital in Europe.

But the annotation which reveals more of White than any other concerns one of the most notorious slums in London's history, the old Westminster Rookery. In his observations concerning the purlieus of Tothill Street, White exercises the bitter irony of the compassionate idealist, painting a vivid picture of poor but honest folk achieving a kind of nobility through suffering:

> Lewisham Street might have been likened to a long, deep trench. It was inhabited by working-class people, poor and with worldly possessions consisting chiefly of children. Although probably out of work for the greater part of their time, the Lewisham Street folk strove to make the best of an uncongenial environment and a debased social condition. They had an inherent love of nature, which impelled them to deck each window with creeping-jennies and three or four (or more) birdcages; and so the flowers bloomed in Lewisham Street and the alley resounded with the songs and chirrupings of the thrush and the bullfinch. Matthew Parker Street too had its residents partial to birds and flowers, but Lewisham Street was a hanging garden and aviary compared with it. And although these byways were ennobled by the names of a bishop and a lord (curious irony), few strangers penetrated into them. The usual visitors were the landlord, the tallyman, the milkman and, on Sundays (even the poor have their luxuries) the winkle-man.

Gradually the moral fervour of the annotations and the attitudes they reveal begin to build up a portrait of a man who fondly believed he was keeping himself to himself. Here are two more which represent other sides to his nature:

Holywell Street was the great resort of the second-hand booksellers, and was a picturesque enough byway; nothing quite like it now exists in London. Wych Street was similar, but had a greater number of old gabled houses, many dating from the sixteenth century. Both streets had numerous shops dealing in articles of an indelicate nature and, as a result, had unsavoury reputations, on which account there was an endeavour to have Holywell Street called Booksellers' Row, but the new name never caught on. The demolition of these streets caused their unsavoury businesses to be distributed through the West End streets, particularly about Leicester Square, a fact that does not say very much for the bye-laws of the metropolis. However, what would have shocked the past generation would not raise a blush among the present one.

For a curiosity in nameplate spelling, the plates identifying St. James's Square at Notting Hill would be hard to beat – except at an Underground station. The Kensington surveyor put one up: 'St. James's Square'. Now, this spelling is absolutely the correct form, according to all the rules and regulations of the King's English, as approved by recognised authorities. Maybe, however, the surveyor had just a doubt about it, so we find close by that there is a nameplate recording: 'St James' Square'. Then, seemingly, he had a doubt about this form of spelling also. He had a third go, and this is what the observant passer-by will come across – 'St. James Square'.

White now emerges in the familiar colours of a Socialist idealist trembling with Ruskinian passion at the spectacle of a great city being desecrated, a pedant who fulminates against the misplacement of an inverted comma, a prig tainted with the kind of puritanism which cannot bring itself to approach any closer to an aroma of moral turpitude than to euphemise it into 'unsavoury'. Do such men, dedicated as they might be, ever have any practical effect on affairs? For all their keenness of scrutiny and fearlessness of reportage, do they ever succeed in stemming the philistine tide? White modestly offers one scrap of evidence in his own behalf. It may cause him to resort yet again to the expediency of euphemism, but he

goes ahead unflinchingly, as he tells the sorry tale of the quadrangle of Somerset House:

Let us turn to the manner in which His Majesty's Office of Works maintained the statue of the present king's ancestor. With an eye to economy, maybe, if with no regard to art, and respect for sovereignty, they converted the plinth of the statue into a – URINAL. The statue stands in the courtyard of a state building that was at one time a palace. Comment is superfluous – even the Bolshevists of Russia would have some regard for the public decency though none for memorials of sovereignty.

Through action taken by the present writer the urinal was removed, Sir Aston Webb, who was approached in the matter, being responsible for this. This little improvement is touched upon here merely to indicate how much the very ordinary Man in the Street can do to effect improvements with respect to the London statues by a little initiative. Whether our memorials be good, bad or indifferent as works of art, the majority of them are generally made infinitely worse by thoughtlessness on the part of the authorities.

A formidable man, and it is no wonder that his masters at London Transport opted for a quiet life and decided to let him go his own way. We can speculate as to where that way led him frequently in the years between 1922 and 1924. Having made a careful study of existing photographs of London bus routes, White marched out into the streets in those three years photographing scenes which had either been photographed before or were about to suffer profound change. He then grouped the photographs into districts, taking great care to pair off photographs of some identical scene before and after the Great War, before and after the replacement of horse by motor car, before and after redevelopment, before and after what he usually regarded as despoliation. There is no question that White's interest was purely topographical, or that his imagination was stirred by impersonal aspects of metropolitan life. He could wax indignant over a vista or a skyline, tremble with moral outrage over architecture, mass, elevation. Only rarely in his notes does he give any indication that those streets about whose welfare he was so solicitous are peopled with Londoners.

And yet, as the reader will discover, it is often humanity rather than its backdrop which engages the eye. Here is the deepest irony of all about White, that a man so preoccupied with the photogenic properties of a city's face should have preserved, by accident, the identical properties of its citizens. The camera shutter clicks, in 1898, or in 1923, and in that lost moment captures the fleeting issues of London street life. In White's record humanity is caught on the wing. Sometimes that humanity is self-consciously aware it is being observed and stares back, outfacing the camera with childlike curiosity. But for the most part it proceeds on its way, intent on its own mysterious business, blissfully unaware that the Recording Angel, in the unlikely disguise of a London Transport clerk, is preserving its image for all time.

Benny Green

'The photographer spoke of Unknown London;
a romantic and bookish phrase.
Most of London is unknown to most Londoners.
It was supposed, too, that when a subject
for a picture was found I could
tell the artist a story about it.
I remembered then how little I know.'
H. M. TOMLINSON

The photographs (apart from occasional pages devoted to special subjects) have been arranged in the form of a tour of central London. The tour commences in the east at Tower Bridge, journeys west through the City into Holborn, hops south to St Paul's, then west again up Fleet Street and the Strand to Trafalgar Square. Down Whitehall to Westminster and Millbank, over to Buckingham Palace, thence to Sloane Square, Chelsea and north to Kensington High Street. The route then turns back eastwards through Knightsbridge, Hyde Park, Piccadilly Circus, up Regent Street, jumps west to Marble Arch, then east again along Oxford Street, finishing up in Bloomsbury. There are many minor excursions off the main route.

Old photographs can be the next best thing to a time machine. But their abilty to transport us seems to reduce in ratio to the degree of conscious selection and arrangement made by the photographer. The photographs in Charles White's albums were never intended to be 'creative'. They were taken as sharp record shots of street locations using a large format plate camera producing glass negatives. The results contain numerous incidents of which the photographer must have been as unaware at the time of shooting as were the subjects of his presence. We have enlarged some of the characters and incidents that fascinate us, but the observant reader will find many more trips on the time machine contained within these pages.

L.E.

A HORSE-DRAWN BUS with a pride of admirers, whose numbers may be due to the fact that the team is standing outside a public house, in Goldhawk Road, Shepherd's Bush. As usual the advertisements run the full gamut from the domestic to the convivial; the cocoa is perhaps for the two small boys poised for a moment behind the pleasing parabola of the outside staircase, while Toole's special Scotch whisky would go down well with the three men, blue-serged and billycocked, their nonchalant leader sporting the modest glint of the watch chain to indicate that these are men of the world who know what time it is. It looks like a dry if overcast day, although the subsequent glories of colour photography might have revealed that over apparently colourless Goldhawk Road on that long-lost morning the London skies were of the subtlest opal grey. The invisible proprietor of the Queen of England public house clearly understands the golden rule of his profession which is that a pub must display bright lights and pretensions to horticulture if it is to draw the customers from their drab households; notice the elaboration of the flower display and the sturdy confidence of the lamp suspended over the doorway.

The most pathetic figure in the composition is the lone rider in the grey topper, frozen in so studied an attitude that he might be a waxwork or a tailor's dummy. He represents one of the gravest problems of omnibus travel of the period, the imminence of rain coupled with an absence of roof. All the bus companies provided waterproof aprons which passengers generally agreed were not waterproof enough. If conditions became too damp, the passenger could always jump off; not so the driver, who was obliged to sit it out. According to Arnold Bennett, who boarded a bus at Piccadilly on a rainswept midnight in January 1899 and characteristically insinuated himself into conversation with the driver, the secret was Cod Liver Oil, a curative so powerful that the driver told Bennett that so far as rain was concerned, 'We gets used to it. But we gets so we *has* to live out of doors. If I got a indoor job I should die. I have to go out for a walk afore I can eat my breakfast.' A walk, perhaps, to an establishment not altogether dissimilar to the Queen of England.

THE ARRIVAL OF the Edwardian
motor-bus brought with it one notorious versified squib:
  What is it that roareth thus?
  Can it be a motor bus?
  Yes, the smell and hideous hum
  Indicat Motorem Bum.
But it brought precious little
change in design. The curve of the
outside staircase remains identical,
even to the angle of the handrail
leading to the still roofless upstairs.
The chief beneficiary seems to be
the driver, who, although still exposed to the elements, at least now
has a roof over his head. The Great
Eastern, one of whose fleet is seen
here about to leave its Leyton
garage, was one of several lesser
companies of the day, although
competition for trade was no longer
quite as raw as in horsedrawn days.
At one time the London General
Omnibus Company had to endure
the rivalry of the London Road
Car Company, which organisation
wittily appropriated the national
flag as a symbol of its brave resist-
ance to oppression. The flag fluttered from a pole to the right of the
driver with the device 'No Mon-
opoly' printed across its colours.
This rivalry was often taken up by
the passengers, whose partisanship
occasionally spilled over into open
warfare. Compton Mackenzie remembered 'what fun it was to ride
on the top of a Road Car bus armed
with peashooters and shoot up the
passengers on the outside of a
General while the drivers raced
one another along the Hammersmith Road. The very horses themselves seemed to enjoy the sport as
their hooves thudded on the wooden
pavement of the road. I still have a
picture in my mind's eye of those
passengers under fire, holding the
collars of their greatcoats over
their ears, their heads bent low.'
  Rumours of High Culture were

carried through Leyton by the
Great Eastern, which advertised
the latest play by Sir Hall Caine.
This represents a distinct decline
in intellectual power from Fry's
Cocoa, for Max Beerbohm has recorded that Caine's reputation was
so lamentable that 'at parties you
could get a laugh by just saying
"Hall Caine . . . "'. A man whose
pointed white beard gave him the
look of an animated peardrop,
Caine specialised for many years
in asking eternal questions of assorted kinds to which, in his inter-
minable plays and novels, he provided the most comically ephemeral
answers.

As LONDON ADAPTS to the internal combustion engine, that urban symbol the Man in the Street gives way to his successor, the Man on the Clapham Omnibus, the archetype whom all politicians ignore at their peril. What the Man on the Clapham omnibus thinks, most ordinary people are thinking everywhere. Read the secrets of his mind and the secrets of *vox populi* are bared. But what does he think? What does he desire? The difficulty of divining his innermost feelings is infinitely complicated by the fact that he is to all intents and purposes invisible – except on those rare unguarded occasions when the casual click of a camera discovers him. In this shot taken in 1921 he is found leaving Clapham Common for the hinterlands of Surrey. As he trudges up the staircase in the wake of matrons, he seems weighed down by the cares of the world and a grey homburg. Is he remembering something he once saw in Flanders? Or is he merely looking for loose change on the stairs? For him, if appearances are anything to go by, life is serious, life is earnest, and while waiting for his bus to arrive, he probably never even spared a glance to the posters behind him hinting at an altogether more carefree world, in which the mysterious Mrs Macdonald hires the local Assembly Rooms for her Easter Carnival Ball, Admission 3/–, and in which the weekend racing sheet names likely winners at twopence per issue.

LONDONERS REMAIN VAGUE enough about their own landmarks to assume, almost without considering it, that Tower Bridge is an adjunct to the Tower itself, part of a medieval package, so to speak. But the bridge, which vies with St Paul's and the Houses of Parliament as the most emblematic of all London structures, is a comparative newcomer. In this photograph, taken in 1890, the construction of the bridge is at exactly the halfway stage, four years work having been completed, with four more still to come. It is that gap between the two banks which renders the scene eerily unreal to the modern eye so absolutely conditioned to seeing the bridge in its completed state, encrusted by history. Victorian pragmatism, allied to delusions of grandeur, dictated that the design should be supervised by two men, Sir John Wolfe Day, the engineer, and Sir Horace Jones, who gave the structure a fake Gothic stone overcoat complete with fairyland turrets and windows. The bascules, each weighing over a thousand tons, were designed to open to allow ships to pass upstream between the Tower and the quaintly named Pickled Herring Stairs. At high tide the bridge's arms stand 140 feet above the water, but by the time of the second photograph, the original footpath running across the arms had long since been closed. Ironically, today the bridge symbolises, not Victorian ingenuity, but neo-Elizabethan obsolescence. The docks in whose midst it was placed now stand derelict or converted to more frivolous uses, although such an idea would have seemed less like blasphemy than lunacy in 1923. To this day the bridge stands over the shifting tides, which ebb rapidly after midday, with the sun, in H. M. Tomlinson's words, 'lowering into London's vapours'.

THE NEW TOWER WHARF at its re-
opening in 1894. From here the
Royal Artillery Company will continue to fire its royal salutes, deton-
ating shells into history against the
background of what V. S. Pritchett
once called a lump of dead history.
Even as this photograph is being
taken, the teenaged shipping clerk
destined to become the poet of the
foreshore is wandering the Thames
wharves gaping at the grandeur of
the great sailing ships. He is H. M.
Tomlinson, who once upon a time
strolled down Tower Hill, past the
entrances to great warehouses: 'We
noticed that each opened vault had
its tutelary cat taking the sun,
crouched at ease on a sufficiency of
food, letting the hours pass. They
showed proper respect for the mel-
lowed merit of their neighbour-
hood, the precincts of the Tower.'
He noted too that it was here-
abouts that the crew of Conrad's
'Narcissus' was paid off, 'swaying
irresolutely and noisily on the
broad flagstones, and then drifting
out of sight', here that Pepys, terri-
fied by a mob of brawling sailors,
turned tail and fled home to the
safety of Seething Lane. Nearby
are those symbols of maritime authority, Trinity House and the P.L.A.,
overseeing the thousands who
work on or for or by the river.
Tomlinson muses: 'Authority looks
down over their heads to the moat
of the Tower, where a garrison continues to post its sentries, and peremptory bugles sound.'

But who are these six soldiers
gathered outside a public house on
some unspecified late Victorian
morning? Certainly not the blowers
of those peremptory bugles. Their
parade dress and swagger sticks
suggest some ceremonial occasion,
perhaps the Diamond Jubilee? The
arm-badge of a castle surmounted
by a sphinx might suggest the
Dorsetshire Regiment, and the
letters RUI on the breast of the central figure's frock-coat would mean
the Indian Army. Some of Kipling's
heroes then, associates of Mul-
vaney, Ortheris and Learoyd, home
for a spot of leave? The only likely
deduction is founded on the absence
of drinking glasses and a general
air of resignation. The six soldiers
are waiting for the pub to open.

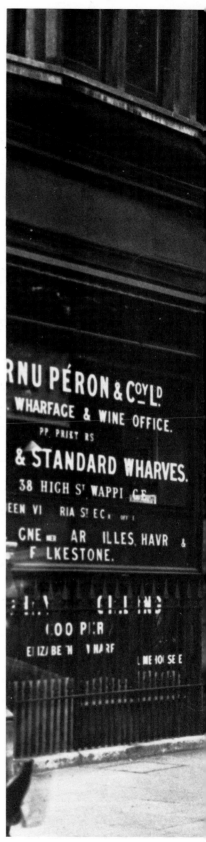

TRINITY SQUARE, just north of the
Tower, seems positively aromatic
with mercantile affairs. The date is
1912, the very year that saw the
construction of the grandiose
Trinity House, headquarters of the
Port of London Authority. This is
a more modest scene. Merchandise
from France has been loaded onto
a cart guarded by a sentry looking
too young for his responsibilities.
Like him, the important-
looking gentleman poised on the
threshold of Catherine Court and
the young clerk to his left, seem
deferential towards the camera.
Only the portly, bowler-hatted,
shirt-sleeved gentleman in the cart
ignores the lens and continues rum-
maging for something in his basket.
The blinkered horse stands
patiently awaiting the call, tactfully ignoring the fact that his re-
lations have recently sprinkled the
road liberally with droppings. It
may be a prosperous enterprise we

are watching, but the management
has certainly been negligent
enough to allow the window to fall
into alphabetical disrepair. We dis-
cern a mysterious thoroughfare
called High Street Wappi, and see
also that no more than the vestigial
remains of the names of Queen
Victoria, Bolougne, Marseilles,
Havre and Folkestone have survived the years.

LIVERPOOL STREET looking west, in 1884; the crowd in the foreground, having spotted the camera, seem instinctively to group themselves in the symmetry of tableaux; the moustachioed policeman pauses in his task of questioning the school-boy, the lady in the cream ensemble turns away from her two more soberly-dressed companions to register her curiosity; the very paper-sellers pause in their chor-eography to look into the camera's eye. London Transport's White was inclined to be sniffy about what had happened to Liverpool Street since the days in the 1820s when it had been 'a respectable avenue, a resi-dential street'. The railways came along in the 1870s to change all that. But exactly how rapid was the tide of change? By 1923 the horses have been put out to grass, and the covered-in omnibuses have lost that swaggering stage-coach aspect. St Mary's Church, directly facing us, suddenly no longer faces us and its situation has been usurped by the inevitable office block. Broad Street Station, built in the 1850s in what Sir John

Betjeman defined as Lombardic style, has been reduced to the usual Portland stone, leaving hidden Lombardic remnants inside. But railway stations mean passengers, hasty assignations, which mean eating houses. The grandly titled Grill Room and Buffet has reverted to the modesty of a dining room, although continuity has been main-tained. But there seems in the later scene to be less time to stand and stare. Or is it simply that this time people hurry to their appointments with destiny, unaware they are being observed?

A GENERATION EARLIER, Dickens, wandering about this district and marvelling at its uncanny sabbath hush, was visited by whimsical fancies concerning the secrets of the heart inscribed on writing pads of absent clerks, and the contents of the wastepaper baskets of the closed and shuttered counting houses. Looking about him at the deserted streets he asked himself:

'Where are all the people who on busy working days pervade these scenes?' But as the new century dawns, the Central London Railway is opening the area to sightseers, churchgoers, holidaymakers. Our fond conception of the City on Sunday as a wasteland inhabited only by pigeons and policemen is destroyed by Charles White's caption: 'Sunday in the City, 1902; the

Bank area shortly after the opening of the Central London railway.' A family of children waits alongside father outside the entrance to the station. The clock on the dome in the foreground indicates twenty-five-past-one; sharp shadows and the absence of overcoats suggest a warm summer day. If only the cameraman had moved his angle a little we might be able to make a more

informed guess as to prevailing weather conditions. One of those whimsicalities which animate the tradition of London concerns the Beadle of the Bank of England, who is authorised to discard his crimson and black overcoat and expose himself in puce and scarlet and gold once the temperature reaches seventy degrees Fahrenheit. City men glance at that Beadle as a casual holidaymaker might read a boarding-house barometer, anxious to know whether the heat they feel is real or imagined. Presumably the Beadle has gone metric since, which is not such a terrible fate as that which befell the Bank of England in the 1920s, when its interior was gutted in the name of some bogus functional theory. Years later this act was mildly described as 'one of the most unbelievable acts of vandalism committed in London in the twentieth century'. But this afternoon nobody suspects what is coming, not even that deeply interested group staring at us from the traffic island, and supervised by a bearded policeman.

THE ROYAL EXCHANGE, outside whose porticoed façade Edwardian City clerks come to munch their lunchtime sandwiches on benches kindly provided. Four of the five buses in the foreground represent a carnival of advertising on behalf of that toilet perquisite whose virtues were transparent, Pear's Soap. The appearance alongside of the name of Gossages is a reminder of the sad oversight by which no considerable Gilbertian versifier ever took advantage of that shop's conjunction with Gorringe's to compose an ode to the beauties of sausages and oranges. All but the boatered, boutonièred chap in the two-tone ensemble are swathed in sober City hues, which is only appropriate for so august a financial clearing in the urban jungle.

In 1923, when the photograph below was taken, looking towards Mansion House, H. V. Morton wrote that the Royal Exchange 'sits in the heart of London with the traffic on all sides, the telephones in every office, the little messages ticking themselves instantly under the Atlantic into Canada, America, South Africa. Through the air go messages that link continent to continent, hemisphere to hemisphere.' It is striking to see how, in the face of the chaos of traffic, even that consummate strategist the Duke of Wellington has been outflanked. At the ceremonial opening of the rebuilt Exchange in 1844, the Iron Duke, or in this case, the Bronze Duke, was unveiled in the presence of its model, who, entering to the strains of 'See The Conquering Hero Comes', calmly examined his own effigy and then walked to the main entrance of the new building, where the ushers, cowed by the eye that had cowed the French, allowed his Grace in even though he had no ticket. In 1923 there he sits, imperfectly accoutred, for the sculptor forgot to provide him with any stirrups.

AT THE SMITHFIELD end of Little Britain on a quiet day in 1912 is a whimsical juxtaposition of God and Mammon. Crowding the gates giving on to the Norman church of St Bartholomew the Great is a stationery shop which even on its own reckoning is a cheap establishment. In Stuart times this was a famous street for bookshops, but by now the literary connections have shrunk to the business of Evans & Witt, purveyors of pens and papers. And over the very threshold of the church there is painted a proclamation regarding the availability of pickled tongues. Hogarth was born here, and Milton once hid here, but now there appears to be no life left in the place. The placards tell us that the king of Sweden is on a state visit, but it is the banner on the far right which confirms the exact date. It blazons the name of Ranji, His Highness the Jam Sahib of Nawanagar, the great Sussex and England cricketer.

By now Ranji's course is almost run. He is in his fortieth year, and this will be his last English season. His appearances are infrequent, and only once has he performed spectacularly enough to justify headlines – in the Championship match between Sussex and Lancashire at Hove – when he and Johnny Tyldesley virtually played each other while the other twenty combatants applauded. Ranji's name on the placard suggests that this photograph was taken on July 24, 1912, the day after his dazzling 176. On the far side of the church entrance are posted details of services, but it is beyond the gate and into the courtyard that the eye yearns to explore. The milky, diffused light, the two lit lamps, the bright faces of the upper windows, and the deserted thoroughfare suggest the longueurs of a summer twilight.

VICTORIAN MERCANTILE London marches back and forth across London Bridge, the causeway leading from suburbia to the City. Clerks and merchants, speculators and messengers, sharepushers and pillars of society, jostle in the race for a better life, unimpeded by the presence on the bridge of more than a few women. One or two commuters march against the tide, but most of the time it is one-way traffic, either to or from Cannon Street Station, the great dispersal point on the road from commerce to domesticity and back again. None of the pedestrians in this photograph are going to work; they dignify the exercise by calling it 'business', and the young clerks, mindful of their status as literate, respectable, coming men, would not consider themselves properly dressed if their white collars and clean cuffs were not augmented by the halfpenny newspaper either flourished in the hand like an officer's cane or folded and tucked under the arm. Cannon Street, the London terminus of the South-Eastern Railway, spills out these thousands every morning and digests them again every evening. Many of the commuters will spend their lunchtimes in personal pursuits, eager to take advantage of Cannon Street's excellent shopping facilities. Here, in smart groceries, businessmen mingle with their book-keepers in the throng for the best butter and china tea. C. H. Rolph remembers that 'one of those grocers in Cannon Street, I forget which, even sold beef dripping in tied-up pudding basins', and, on a more decorous level: 'These City grocers would still weigh out tea and sugar by hand, making conical sugar bags from strong blue paper; and they still knocked a pound of butter into shape with wooden platters.'

Such modest sentimentality was not for Charles White, who had only to see a Thames bridge to begin flinging brickbats at his betters. He felt that, 'during the first fifty years of its existence, the L.C.C. has adopted a dilatory attitude towards the Thames bridges, which is largely responsible for a good deal of the chaos in London traffic'. White felt that 'the Albert and Wandsworth bridges are quite useless for modern traffic', and that Lambeth Bridge was 'very much a failure from the traffic point of view'. He even regretted that London Bridge had been rebuilt between 1886–94, and waxed poetic in his recollections of the old one: 'If you, good reader, would see Old London Bridge as it stood in all its glory, with its chapel, its gatehouses, its waterworks, its houses and shops, its piers and starlings, its drawbridge, spare a moment to turn aside from the bustle of living London and, in the basement of the London Museum, gaze upon the model of the wondrous old bridge that gave a crossing of the Thames in the London of the past. And give a thought to the good people, long forgotten, who of their charity provided the funds of the Bridge House.'

LONDON BRIDGE B·1065

WORKADAY LONDON HURRIES by,
en route to its assignations with
destiny without so much as a glance
at the destruction of one of the most
forbidding structures ever erected
in any city. Newgate Prison, built
by the City Surveyor George Dance
the Younger between 1770–78, was
a place of such overbearing penal
aspect that no writer ever seems to
have done full justice to it. The
Victorian A. H. Beavan said it possessed, 'with the exception of the
Tower, a record fuller of dark
shadows than any existing edifice'.
Boswell was so depressed by his
visit that the recollection, 'hung
on my mind like a black cloud',
which persisted so vividly that
later that night he had to ask his
barber to read him to sleep. James
Bone, writing from memory, described, 'the nightmare iron door
on the front wall made to imitate
stone; the leering old Caroline
statues of Flora and Ceres and
those other stony virgins who used
to stand in niches on the terrible
wall, the little spiky gates, the
whole menacing thing'. But by far
the most celebrated description of
Newgate occurs in *Oliver Twist*
when Dickens depicts Fagin's last
night in the condemned cell. When
the prison was finally demolished,
that cell was incorporated into the
basement of Lancaster House. At
the sale of relics, Lord George
Gordon's cell went for £5, Jack
Sheppard's grating for £7 10s. Some
of the remaining stones were re-
deployed when the Old Bailey was
built on the site. There are other
reminders of the bad old days. On
the first two mornings of each new
session, Old Bailey judges carry
flowers and walk over a herb-strewn
floor, in memory of the noisome
fumes which once caused gaol fever.
As for our pedestrians going about
their business, they seem to be ignoring the demolition with the in-
difference of the innocent.

Only those travellers on the
upper deck of the bus trotting to
its familiar destination of Nestle's
Milk seem interested in the passing
of a great landmark. But neither
they nor anyone else suspect the
presence of the true star of the pro-
ceedings, whose actions endow the
moment with the glibness of
parable: the great prison crumbles,
but humdrum life endures. On the
third floor of the Viaduct public
house, that archetypal Londoner,
the Unknown Scullion, is shining
a bedroom window. Or could it be
that having glimpsed the camera,
she is enjoying a momentary diversion by giving its owner a friendly
wave? Whatever her motives on
this lost morning in 1902, she is the
nameless heroine of this book.

MOST OF THE EARLY photographs in White's collection disclose a world going about its business unaware it is being observed. But here, in the north-west corner of St Paul's Churchyard in 1880 there is something charmingly self-conscious. The photographer might almost have arranged the groupings, so quaint does the attitudinising of the people seem: the messenger boy scratching his ear, the white-coated street cleaner standing easy, the man in the road pausing in the act of pushing his wheelbarrow into history, the bowler-hatted trio on the kerb-edge, the well-to-do couple who look as if they have just sneaked out of the pub, the top-hatted gent poised in the doorway, and that matriarch, formidable as your mother-in-law, armoured in black bombasine. They seem less like Londoners than supernumeraries in some forgotten operetta, awaiting the orchestral cue to break into a rhythmic strut and dispense the latest Leslie Stuart tune. One building, just out of the photo, suffered a sad if patriotic fate. Spence's Furniture shop was demolished to make way for a stand for Victoria's Diamond Jubilee, and nobody ever managed to raise the money to rebuild it.

The two views of the west end of Cheapside are a perfect example of how London contrives to deface itself. In 1875 the buildings serve as a frame for a superb view of the Cathedral; nobody disturbs the reveries of Sir Robert Peel. Forty-eight years later retail trade is attracting the crowds, the stately old house has been replaced by a clothing shop, and that sapling has flourished so prodigiously as to have ruined the view of the Cathedral. But human drama has its compensations. That lady stepping out into the road with arm outstretched, who or what has she seen that lends such urgency to her gesture? It is certainly nothing to do with Sir Robert, who will one day tire of the rising tide of commerce lapping about his feet and remove himself to a park nearby. Even this will prove too hectic for him, and in 1971 he will end predictably at the Police College in Hendon.

FOR ALL THE ECCLESIASTICAL overtones of its title, St Paul's Churchyard, seen here in the south-west
corner, is not a churchyard but a
street, surrounding the cathedral
from which it takes its name. Standing at the head of Cheapside, it
offers some admirable views of
Wren's masterpiece, but that is not
why these people are passing
through on this warm sunshine
day. White stucco in Dean's Court
is dappled with sunlight; probably
such happy weather is bad for business at Mr J. A. Kensit's truth emporium. Mr Kensit, proselytiser in
the cause of the Protestant Truth
Society, is currently peddling his
book, *What I Saw in Rome*, and to
make sure that his supporters see
the same things he did, the book
carries 'many illustrations'. But
business could be brisker. On the
first floor the paper merchants
have gone; above, someone would
seem to be anticipating events by
offering of all things on this day in
1923, 'Brunsviga Calculators'. But
today it is humanity's turn to be
upstaged by the animal kingdom.
In the left foreground the stark
shadow of the back of a van
blackens an oblong of roadway. By
a fluke of alignment the white horse
attached to this van is patiently
awaiting orders, and has achieved
such perfect stasis that its un-
smudged reflection creates the
illusion across the road of a horse
standing in a shop window.

In the north-west corner (far left),
Evans's Restaurant seems to be
doing much better business than
Mr Kensit, the pleasures of the
flesh overcoming those of the spirit,
even under the shadow of the great
Cathedral. But then the cathedral
has also been the subject of some
alarmingly unsanctified specu-
lations, the oddest of which came
from the Reverend C. L. Dodgson,
who in 1895 had written to Lord
Salisbury suggesting that 'men
should be on watch, day and night,
for the first symptoms of a fire, and
then, by being in electric communication with the fire-engine stations,
rouse all those who are nearest'. In
developing his theme, Dodgson suggested the top of St Paul's as the
perfect vantage point, with an observation station provided with 'a
minute map of the district and a
good telescope'. Salisbury replied
that he would take up the sug-
gestion with someone connected
with the Fire Brigade. Posterity
awaits the outcome.

L.S.&.P.C2.

St martin's-le-grand in the summer of 1914. Ladies in picture hats brave the perils of life on the upper deck. The one wearing the white hat appears to be following the progress of the man in the panama crossing the road carrying a rolled umbrella in one hand and a newspaper in the other. An interesting, bearded, bespectacled man, faintly alien and Conradian in demeanour; perhaps he is cogitating on the practicalities of blowing up Greenwich Observatory, or even the building he is walking away from, the General Post Office on the east side of the street. Originally the Post Office was a two-storey building with a grandiose Ionic portico, but a few years before this photograph was taken, a third storey had been added, defacing the line of the original. But the point was academic; in 1912 the demolition men moved in. The hansoms clop by, and in the foreground that newspaper seller obligingly tells us what was thought to interest the average Londoner in the summer of 1904. The Japanese admiral Togo is proceeding with his plan to sink the Russian navy. In the following May he will blow thirty-three of their thirty-five ships out of the water, but for the moment he is content merely to blockade Port Arthur. It will be the first time an Asian force has defeated a European power, and the sweet reward for the Japanese will be a naval treaty with Britain. No wonder the Czarina is not feeling well.

But Fleet Street has the right priorities. The leading item on the placard concerns cricket, and tells us which paper the vendor is selling. In the previous summer the Middlesex and England batsman Pelham Warner had been invited to write weekly articles by the editor of the *Westminster Gazette*, J. A. Spender. The *Westminster*, among the most influential of Liberal organs, was known as the 'Sea-Green Incorruptible' because of the colour of the paper on which it was printed. It finally expired, with the old Liberal Party, soon after the end of the Great War. But on this morning in 1904, nobody is thinking of war. The only explosions in London's thoughts are those being made by Mr Brock's fireworks at Crystal Palace. There had been Brock fireworks at Crystal Palace since 1866, and they were to continue until 1910. Londoners would always retain their childlike appetite for the detonations of Chinese Fliers, Flying Pigeons, Niagaras of Fire, Fiery Whirlwinds, Golden Rain, Maroons and Jewel Fountains.

LUDGATE HILL LOOKING west from St Paul's, 1923. Anyone with money in his pockets, or, like the man in the right foreground, who carries it around in a suitcase, can buy anything he pleases here, from gloves to filing systems. He can have his teeth pulled out at Goodman's the dentist, or his hair pulled out next door by the new electric system. If either of those experiences should happen to kill him, he can trot posthumously across the road and take his choice of wreaths and crosses. If on the other hand he survives, he can purchase a remedial cup of scalding, orange-coloured tea round the corner in Lyons' teashop, whose façade on the right-hand side of the road is just recognisable. Or he could take a ride in that taxi cab, in the hope that its elegantly booted driver will heed the sign on the central lamp-post advising people to drive slowly. A lady performs a neat time-step as she disembarks from a bus about to

disappear off the bottom left of the photograph. As for Queen Anne, attended by stony young ladies from England, Ireland, North America and India, she studies the train in the middle distance as it crosses Ludgate Bridge belching out secret maps in white smoke. Her Majesty has her back to the Cathedral, and at one time, a wine and spirits shop immediately before her, a fluke which inspired some of the finest poetry of her reign:

> Brandy Nan, Brandy Nan,
>   you're left in the lurch
> With your face to the gin shop,
>   your back to the church.

It was this statue to which Henry James came running the moment he arrived in London, impelled 'by the way two lines of "Henry Esmond" repeated themselves in my mind as I drew near the masterpiece of Sir Christopher Wren: "The stout, red-faced" woman whom Esmond had seen tearing after the staghounds over the slopes at Windsor was not a bit like the effigy which turns its stony back on St Paul's and faces the coaches struggling up Ludgate hill. As I looked at Queen Anne over the apron of my hansom, she struck me as very small and dirty, and the vehicle ascended the mild incline without an effort – it was a thrilling thought that the statue had been familiar to the hero of the incomparable novel. All history appeared to live again, and the continuity of things to vibrate through my mind.'

It would be pleasant to think that the small boy being led by the hand across the road towards us has just been fed in the teashop, and is now so replete with crumpets and eclairs just delivered by the Lyons van behind him, and is so impressed by the cosmopolitan implications of the word 'Maison' on its front, that he is now in a suitably receptive mood to be vouchsafed a religious experience in the cathedral.

TWO STREET SCENES at Blackfriars Station demonstrating the startling contrasts in stylishness of horse-drawn traffic. The team in the foreground humps a cargo of empty vegetable baskets towards the Embankment, while the bus carries its cargo of boatered young men across Blackfriars Bridge. A bowler-hatted man bicycles earnestly in the opposite direction. In the second photograph a street-cleaner scoops up his harvest of horse-droppings (see also overleaf).

Only two men (below) are conscious of the camera, and they form part of a remarkable centrepiece, a perfect shot of one of the most elegant forms of transport ever evolved. Disraeli dubbed them the gondolas of London, and the poet Richard Le Gallienne, sighting them in the Strand at night, wrote:

Like dragonflies the hansoms
    hover
With jewelled eyes to catch
    the lover.

In 1900 there were 25,000 hansoms plying for hire in the streets of London. By 1912 only 400 were left, and by the 1920s they were antiquities only to be glimpsed outside the Café Royal, or perhaps late at night at the Garrick Club. Queen Victoria bought her own hansom for £200 in 1887; her son ran around town in one through the 1880s; Sherlock Holmes was more than partial to its amenities when in pursuit, and actually tipped a driver half a sovereign for services rendered in *The Hound of the Baskervilles*. Indeed, as Holmes would have said, the subject bears closer investigation.

'The passing of the hansom was a peculiar loss, the tall, delicately poised carriage, shining black, with the driver commanding cab and horse from his lofty seat, and the slender whip rising high above all, was one of the most decoratively satisfying things that London has ever produced. It was like an invention from the beautifully attenuated art of Whistler, who always brought a hansom into his lithographs when he could.'
    James Bone; *London Echoing*

'The cab slowly patrols Regent Street; the cabby, with trained eye, scans the pavements; the swell, with a flick of the eyelid, conveys the message which the cabby instantly translates into action. The cab spins round in its own length as a result of an adroit movement by the horse, clearly an equine genius, and the cab is at the kerb. With skill acquired only by experience, the swell is inside in three steps and sinks back on the cushioned seat. The cab sways luxuriously on its ample springs. The cabby opens the little door in the roof and a few cryptic words suffice to send the gondola of the streets on its way. The horse progresses with long strides, and the cab skims lightly on its tall slender wheels as if travelling on air. Rubber tyres and wood paving made its wheels silent; the familiar 'click-clock' of the horse's hooves and the bells musically tinkling on the horse's neck provided the signature tune of London town. There was an elegant, rakish, up-all-night air about a hansom. No wonder a lady was never expected to travel in one unattended.'
Frederick Willis; *101 Jubilee Road*

'These poor jog-trotting survivals (as we think them) seemed then to be prodigies of perfect springing, elimination of friction, balance, comfort, and speed. We had hardly started, the horse's feet clumping merrily, the wood-and-glass apron-doors shut cosily, the body jigging with the resilience of an air-cushion, the bells ringing, than we drew up before the dim-lit portico, sprang out to assist our whitely voluminous lady to alight, rang a bell or watched a latchkey turning, shook a reluctant parting hand, heard a door bang, and trotted off again into the empty dim-lit streets. It is thrilling to get in, thrilling to jog along with the horse's back and ears in front, and the animal steam rising; thrilling to hear the jingle, the creak of harness, to see the shafts wobbling in the harness, to be aware of that tough old man on the box behind and above the dark compartment, who suddenly will slacken his horse's pace, lift the little high shutter, and ask for a specific direction.'
    J. C. Squire; *A London Reverie*

MEANWHILE AT Holborn Circus, on the southern side by Thavies Inn, yet another form of horse transport is on display. The year is 1874, the London heyday of the French artist Gustave Doré, whose sketches of London low life, much of it wrapped in fog, were much in vogue. There was a climate of opinion which felt that Doré's later, sacred paintings were bad compared to the secular lithographs of his youth. Walter Sickert took exception to this theory, insisting that each were as bad as the other, and that Doré 'touched nothing that he did not spoil.' In this photograph, not only is Christ leaving the Praetorium, but the Prince Consort, up there on his stone horse, is leaving his senses. As White puts it the Prince is shown 'in Field Marshal's uniform, committing a grave breach of military etiquette, saluting by waving his cocked hat.'

HOLBORN IN 1897, west of Leather Lane, showing the street poised on the brink of the new century. On the left, demolition is almost complete. The walls and windows of Ridler's Family Hotel are already posted with fond farewells. Soon the pickaxes will be hacking away at the bag shop and the ramparts of Gamages will begin to rise. Among the casualties will be a name prominent in the annals of the minor pleasures of life. Gatti's was synonymous with having a good time. Its modest café in Holborn was a mere outpost of more spectacular enterprises further west. The firm's beer house had already moved over to make way for the Tivoli, but at Charing Cross Gatti's own music hall still thrived. It was much beloved of Kipling,

who once claimed that he could look out of the window of his rooms in Villiers Street 'through the fanlight of Gatti's entrance across the street, almost on to its stage.' In one of the most affecting cameos ever written about London life, James Bone described Gatti's café room as, 'the middle-class house for doing yourself well on a night out in London. I think of it as the home of the lonely man. On a Saturday night you would see them, each sitting under a hat-tree smoking a meditative cigar, thinking of the old days when supper at Gatti's was an adventure, and of lost friends, and a scattered family and how it would have been different if the wife had lived. I remember sitting next to one such lonely man on a Derby race night, and he told me he always came to Gatti's on Derby night and ate a steak, drank a pint of beer and went home to Streatham Hill by a late bus.'

THE NORTH SIDE OF Holborn. As we look westwards on a day in 1923, we watch office workers striding towards lunch, their numbers swelled by City men come to shop. Those two pipe-smokers in the left foreground pause in their plotting to regard us. Behind them, a man peers into the windows of Thomas Wallis, perhaps with instructions from a suburban wife to bring home a dozen damask dinner napkins in time for tonight's little supper party. Probably he will buy the wrong thing, having missed an essay written just the other day by A. G. Gardiner asserting that male shoppers are amateurs: 'They not only do not know the ropes; they do not know there are any ropes to know.' Nor does window-reconnaissance help; Gardiner again: 'Shop windows are no more like the insides of shops than a company's prospectus is like its balance-sheet.' Across the road Dobbin rests between the shafts of a London and N. W. Railway cart, directing his blinkered gaze at the camera.

Close by stands the giant emporium of Walter Gamage, son of a Herefordshire farmer, who began with a tiny shop in 1878 which grew into one of the most renowned stores in the world. If those workers care to wander inside, there they will find multifarious symbols of the escape they dream of, from explorers' tables and mosquito nets to collapsable urinals. Specialising in Mail Order, and boosting itself as 'The People's Popular Emporium', Gamages is now most famous for the legions of young men who emerge from its doors wearing the items so proudly paraded by P. G. Wodehouse's Clarence Chugwater: 'Flat-brimmed hat, coloured handkerchief, flannel shirt, a bunch of ribbons, a haversack, football shorts, brown boots, a whistle and a hockey stick'. Gamages' status as outfitters to the Boy Scout movement is matched by its fame as purveyor of teddy bears and, for slightly older children, motor bikes. This side of the business is so successful that Walter, when he dies, will lie in state in the Motoring Department, guarded, like some mechanized Napoleon, by his marshals the salesmen.

Such romance as this tableau evokes is quite eclipsed by the gothic rhetoric of the spires of the Prudential Assurance building, pointing up to the place where every policyholder must at last go. But this temple consecrated to the glory of Compound Interest Everlasting, is a cuckoo in the nest of English Literature, a status feebly acknowledged on the left of its gateway, where as Una Pope-Hennessy writes, 'a small bust of Dickens cowers'. Until 1895 here stood Furnival's Inn, to which Dickens moved, and where, 'sans tables, sans curtains, sans french polish', he wrote *The Pickwick Papers*. But nothing in this scene gives any hint that not so long ago miracles were wrought in this street.

LOOKING EAST ALONG Fleet Street on a bright sunlit day in 1880, with the awnings of the shops on the north side swelling out over the pavement like giant parasols. Imperial hints are vouchsafed by the building advertising the Toronto Globe and her sister journals including the Weekly Advertiser. Four years later Chas. Baker, purveyor of grey flannel suits and black brogues to generations of schoolboys, looks across the street to the rival hatters next door to Jacob Townsend of sarsaparilla fame. The hatter, pioneer trade unionist, by now far along the stony road to the Closed Shop, can knock up a fiver a week working piece-rates, cooks his dinner on the premises in ovens provided by the management, and conducts his affairs so well that the most eloquent of his brethren, Frederick Willis, writes of the trade as 'a little republic that was as near justice, honour and fair play as mortals can ever hope to get.' A hint of conviviality is conveyed by the hoarding for Promenade Concerts, by now a traditional feature of London life. Forty years earlier they had been introduced by the Parisian eccentric Louis Jullien, who aspired to immortality by planning to set the Lord's Prayer to music – 'Imagine the song copy, Music by Jullien, Words by Jesus Christ' – and got it by meriting a mention in Gilbert's libretto for 'Patience'.

In the earlier scene, a quartet performs the quaint choreography of a moment. While the lady in the striped shawl, unmindful of her resemblance to Charley's Aunt, swishes on towards Ludgate Hill, the boy scooping up horsedung seems, through a trick of perspective, to be playing leapfrog with the Invisible Man. The shirt-sleeved youth feels in his weskit pocket

with the debonair flourish of Sam
Weller, while before him a sternly
preoccupied man crosses the road,
his knees about to buckle under
the weight of that imposing helmet.
He bears a certain resemblance to
Henry Irving, or perhaps some
Trollopean divine in mufti, intent
on discovering what the *Catholic
Times* has been saying about him.

Four years later the pair pausing
en route to the sarsaparilla headquarters sport high toppers and
Forsytean whiskers; there is a candour about their gaze dangerously
close to aggression. The younger
man shading his eyes looks much
friendlier, but perhaps that too is
to do with millinery. Willis reminds
us that a gentleman in these man-
nered times has to perform so much
hat-doffing that brims require heavy
reinforcing to take the strain.

FLEET STREET, 1878, looking east towards the obsolescent flourish of Temple Bar. This photograph is something of a valedictory, because Wren's arch is at last about to disappear. Later this year it will be removed to the hinterlands of rural Essex, where, in the grounds of Theobald's Park, it will gradually sink into the unbarbered weeds, its façades scarred with grafitti. But now, in 1878, the town is tired of the Arch, which is an impediment to the traffic clattering both ways along the cobbled road. Wooden shutters protect the shop-fronts; outside that public house stand three prospective drinkers, while just behind them the window-cleaner gives a new meaning to the journalistic dream of climbing the ladder of Fleet Street. Between the men and the Arch, horse-drawn traffic approaches like a dark rumour.

In the days before the discovery that its keystone was out of perpendicular, and its subsequent banishment, Temple Bar served a functional purpose. Behind that upstairs window laboured the clerks of Child's Bank, an organisation which had once nurtured the accounts not only of William and Mary, but also of Cromwell and Nell Gwyn, surely the most slapstick juxtaposition in the history even of banking. Two years after the removal of the arch, No. 17 Fleet Street was revelling in juxtaposition of a different kind, with a king and his chancellor sharing star billing over a barber's shop.

By 1923 MR CARTER's modest establishment has been redeveloped with such relentless Tudor fervour that there is no longer any need to proclaim the name of that king and his chancellor. We can no longer distinguish what Mr Carter's prices are; who removed that splendid lamp on which his tariff was painted? The post-war world appears to be in a great hurry. Even that man with hands in pockets is moving fast; even the two men passing the time of day on the street corner do not seem likely to pass very much of it. There is not a bare head in sight, which may explain why poor old Carter has given up on the wig-making side of the business.

Back in 1880, things were different. Everyone had time to stand and stare, the rival attractions being the sensational photographs on display in the windows of the Dundee Advertiser, and our camera. How obligingly the façades of the buildings convert themselves into hoardings, telling us the circulation of *The People's Friend*, the desirability of Mr Davey's advertising facilities, the location of the offices of 'The Artist', and where the prints of William Reeves may be seen. But the most homely news of all is conveyed by Craig's Oyster Rooms, where, we are told, hot fish is available 'from 12 to 12', and Kent Natives are on display in the window, with plenty of Bass, Pale Ale and Guinness to wash them down. Two of the white-aproned waiters have come to the door and are peeping round it, curious to catch a glimpse of the Man of the Year 2000, leaving us to guess at the import of that clearly derisory remark being made by the young man, hands in pockets, addressing his companions outside Mr Reeves' shop without taking his eyes off us.

FLEET STREET IN 1923, celebrated for two institutions, newsprint and conviviality. For every great publishing enterprise in its purlieus, there are at least twenty public houses, taverns and wine bars. Considering the vast numbers employed in the newspaper industry who suffer from its occupational disease of acute thirst the moment they arrive at work, it seems an eminently sensible arrangement. But Fleet Street is a generic term rather than a place; most of the Press barons lurk down side streets north and south, in Fetter and Shoe Lanes, in Whitefriars and Bouverie Streets. The glittering glass façade of the *Daily Express* building will not rise for another nine years, the stony face of the *Daily Telegraph* for another seven. Appearances are deceptive. James Bone, charting the agricultural overtones of the street, claims in the year of this photograph that it has 'more moths and butterflies than any other place except Covent Garden'; early morning printers emerging from the catacombs having put the paper to bed and intent on following suit themselves, still see flocks of Kentish sheep waddling through on their way to Islington Market. A few yards east of Fetter Lane survives one of the great Victorian institutions, Anderton's Hotel, famous for smoking concerts and the ritual of freemasonry. Here transpontine cricket clubs attend annual dinners, sitting among the rumpled napery till the small hours, recalling the good old days before the war and thinking wistfully of what might have been. Those two men crossing the road in front of the cyclist, are they leader writers, perhaps, planning an essay on the honesty of Stanley

Baldwin or the integrity of Ramsay
Macdonald, or the treasurer and
Hon. Sec. of the Prevention of
Premature Burial Society, off to
negotiate terms for the annual
dance at Anderton's? Whatever
their purpose, Anderton's will offer
them exquisite service, for it is the
last London hotel to preserve a
dying and curiously touching Victorian courtesy, the provision of
bedroom slippers for all its customers. Thirteen years later its
thoughtfulness will not save it
from the bulldozers.

MAY 1906. AN ARROW bus pauses
in the Fulham Road on its journey
to the West End. The Danish ballerina Adeline Genée is nearing
the end of her reign as the star of
the Empire ballets, where she has
been turning the heads of audiences
and critics since 1897. Three months
before this photograph was taken,
A. B. Walkley of *The Times* saw
her in 'Cinderella', praising her
with his customary condescention
for 'the charm of native, even
homely simplicity'. In May 1906
Max Beerbohm reviewed her in
'Coppelia' and damned her with
what must be the faintest praise
any ballerina can ever have received
when he said: 'She was born a
comedian, and a comedian she
remains.' In 1907 rumours of her
impending departure spread panic
through the ranks. Bernard Shaw
roused himself to see her dance, and
Walkley, his patrician soul mortified

at the thought of so exquisite if homely an artist going to America, became quite hysterical. Likening her predicament there to that of 'a philosopher at a barbarian court', he searched for ways to keep her in England: 'Is it too late to buy her off? Perhaps another First Folio would do it. London without Genée will be a mere huddle of pedestrians, a benighted place where tiptoing is only known by hearsay. If and when Genée departs she will have to leave London her white satin shoes, to be deposited in the British Museum'. But Genée never strayed far from British theatrical life. In 1915 Arnold Bennett, who had writhed in provincial ecstasy sixteen years earlier at her tremors of strange tints, her tantalizing veils and her mists of iridescent light, was more prosaic after visiting the Coliseum: 'She danced old-fashionedly well amid rotten scenery.' Beerbohm had

once described her art as 'light and liberal', a phrase whose accidental political overtones were echoed in an unfortunate way in 1921 when she danced with Margot Asquith. Born in 1878, she outlived them all, Shaw, Bennett, Beerbohm, Walkley, admirers and detractors alike, remaining active as a teacher of the balletic arts into extreme old age. It is doubtful if many of the passengers on this Fulham omnibus were destined ever to cast eyes on the Genée obituaries, which did not appear until 1970.

Unlike Miss Genée, the ladies who became bus conductresses during the Great War had to be provided with winter *and* summer uniforms, but were spared the heavier work of actually building the buses. In 1911 the workyard of the London General in Holloway was the place where spokesmen for the industry were able to practice

their craft. In the photograph the men appear to be constructing a bus but are in imminent danger of being frustrated by the man in the foreground who has decided to run amok with a sledge-hammer.

THE STRAND BY St Mary le Strand. Ten minutes past four on an afternoon in 1886. At the high noon of empire the upper decks of the buses reflect the proud gloss of toppers, under which heads are buzzing at the thought that Mr Gladstone's ministry is about to take its leave. If and when it does, committed Liberals may drown their sorrows in Short's Wine Bar, while equally committed Tories can toast Lord Salisbury alongside them, perhaps also taking advantage of the offer of 'Hot Joints'. Further west, beyond the frame of the photograph, lies one of Charles White's favourite places, Lowther Arcade, which was to be wiped out as the new century arrived. Every time he thought of the loss, White was overcome by tender recollections of childhood days, although even as he was swept away on the warm tide of nostalgia, he still retained enough command to take a few side-swipes, at interlopers, at commercial interests, even at the reader:

'What middle-aged or elderly Londoner – the real Londoner, not the provincial importation – does not recall the brown-coated, top-hatted beadle who, in all the awful

majesty of resplendent livery and whiskers, chivied from the Arcade the ragged urchins who stole in and gazed with wistful eye upon the goodly array of toys and listened to the music of the humming-tops. Then there were the Boxing Day sales – the children's Saturnalia – when young London came in from all the streets around and brought the damaged toys at rock-bottom prices. But we do digress – and so would *you*, if you had known the Lowther Arcade. Coutts emerged like an ogre from the dirty, grimy buildings across the way and soon the elysium of the young folk became a memory.'

Looking east from Somerset House, 1923. It is striking that everything in this picture fades before the accidental glories of that

wall on the north side (enlarged overleaf). An interesting essay, this, on the transcience of everything except commerce. All those men hurrying along the pavement, the motor car so carefully keeping to the left *and* right sides of the road, most of the bricks and mortar, all dead and gone, long since consigned to the forgotten past. But not the commercial enterprises so modestly advertising themselves on that wall. Bass, Nestles, Worthington, Watneys, HP Sauce, Rowntrees, Gilbeys, *The News of the World*, all still thriving. The message delivered by that wall seems to be that those who yearn for immortality must become chocolate-eating, hard-drinking bill hoarders who enjoy reading about themselves in the sensational press.

Holywell and Wych Streets, western threshold of Clare Market, one of the most notorious of all Victorian rookeries. It is a summer morning in 1900 and for all their relaxed demeanour, the locals know that their world is under imminent sentence of death, doomed to be swept away by the Kingsway-Aldwych Improvement Scheme. The loss will distress a thousand Georgian reminiscers, who will recall Holywell Street as a browser's paradise, a narrow squalid cavalcade of books, many of them of a faintly scurrilous nature. White's tight-lipped disapproval of the 'indelicate nature' of this trade is no more than panic in the face of Maria Monk and the Heptamaron, but even he concedes to Holywell Street a certain picturesqueness and to Wych Street the possession of some sixteenth-century gabled houses.

There is also the little matter of the four theatres that will be casualties of the redevelopment: the Globe, the Olympic, the Strand, and the Opera Comique, original home of the Gilbert-and-Sullivan operas. James Bone mourned the passing of Wych Street's 'Caroline picturesqueness and bawdry', and Fred Willis remembered the odd habit of the Holywell residents who stuck poles out of their windows from which fluttered their wet washing, as though celebrating 'a pageant of poverty'. So scabrous was the reputation of the district that after demolition, respectable mercantile London hesitated to move in. The levelled area became a meadow scattered with wild flowers, which were at last buried under the sobriety of *The Morning Post* and the gaiety of The Gaiety.

'THE LAST DRINK', a tableau of such affecting sentimentality that the coachman may well be shedding a surreptitious tear. The three-tier facilities of the Metropolitan Drinking Fountain and Cattle Trough Association, lower for cats and dogs, upper for horses, top at the side for humans, will soon follow Holywell Street into oblivion.

IT IS NOW 1903. Holywell Street, Wych Street, Clement's Inn – all of them are now consigned to memory – creating one of the most valuable building sites in the world. On the inevitable hoardings, Nestles and Cerebos vie for attention with the promise of a bandstand. And because of the chaos of demolition, the Strand at St Clement Danes has no pavements, a fact which appears to disturb neither the top-hatted, wing-collared gent striding towards the camera, nor the horses plodding along behind him, carrying their passengers to a destination announced on the bus's front as Nestles Milk.

Three more years have passed. The arid wastes of one of the most boring streets in central London are beginning to take shape. As we look north along Kingsway towards Euston, we can see the old and the new still jostling for attention. Technology has already wrought the miracle of subterranean trams, but the horse and cart still prevails, while on the right of the picture an ancient dispensary blinks in the unaccustomed light of its new exposure. London has waited a long time for this new section, so long in fact that the original name, Queensway, had to be dropped when Victoria died, and Kingsway substituted in honour of the monarch who will soon officially open it.

LONDON COUNTY COUNCIL
KINGSWAY.
FOR PARTICULARS OF
BUILDING SITES
TO be LET on LEASE for 99 YEARS
Apply to
THE VALUER TO THE COUNCIL.
9, Spring Gardens, S.W.

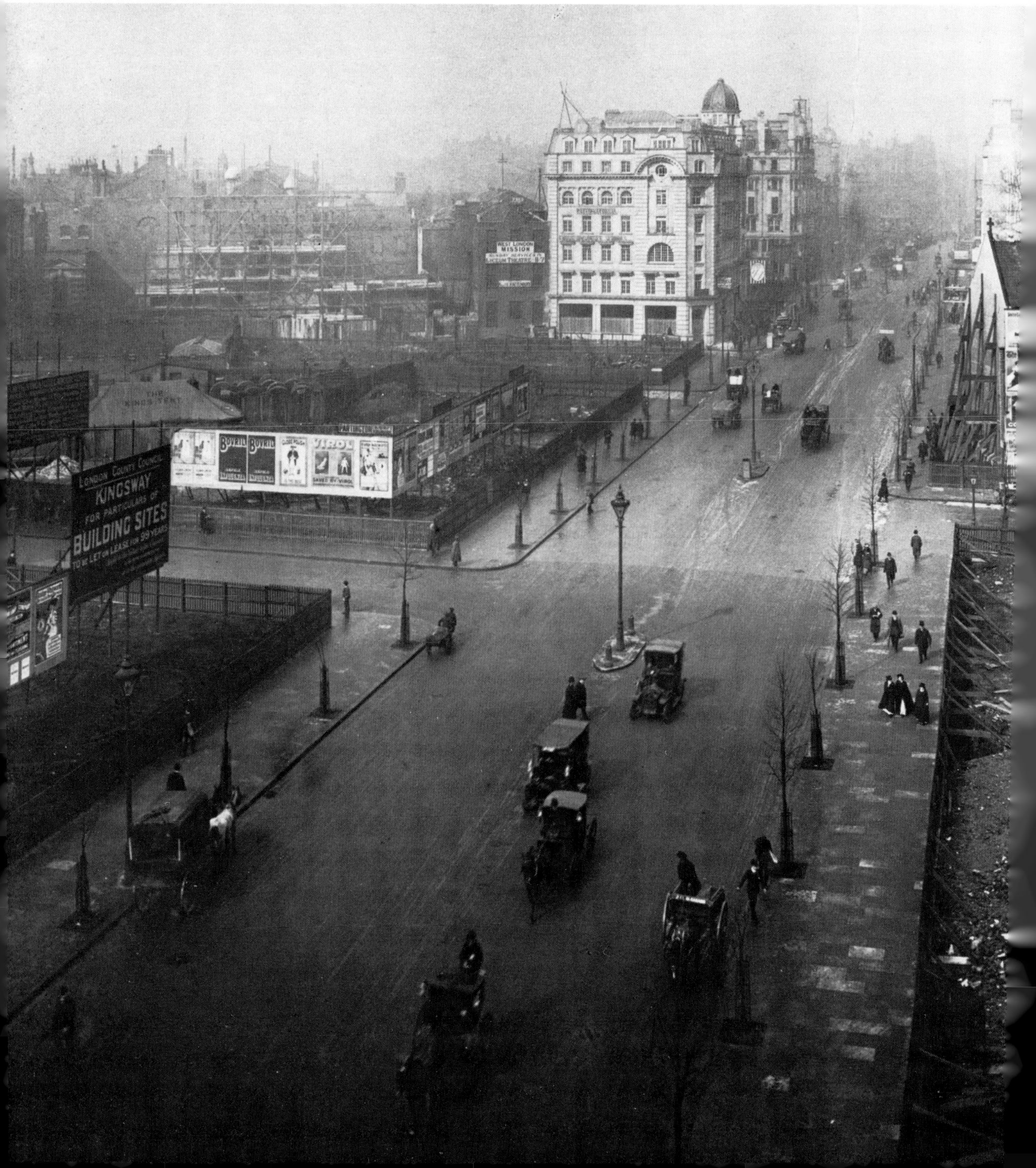
KINGSWAY
BUILDING SITES
BOVRIL
BOVRIL

NONE OF THE PRINCIPALS in this photograph (right), neither the party of young ladies jigging merrily east along the Aldwych, nor the man in the boater running an expert eye over them, nor even the relaxed character sitting against a bollard on the traffic island, have any reason to suspect that one of the greatest careers in the history of popular literature is about to take off. It is a day in 1906. The Kingsway Improvement Scheme remains incomplete; the empty site of the Wardorf-to-be gives the Aldwych Theatre the chance to deploy its west wall as a sandwich board, on which it is announced that Ellaline Terris and Seymour Hicks are starring in a new show. 'The Beauty of Bath' would be totally forgotten today, except for the inclusion in its score of a song called 'Mr Chamberlain', whose lyrics poked good-natured fun at the apostle of Tariff Reform. So frequent were Joe Chamberlain's indiscretions, and so widespread his fame, that the lyrics of the song were amended weekly to fit the latest developments. This unending topicality required no further labours from the composer, an obscure young American called Jerome Kern, but placed on the versifier a burden which the young man in question was only too delighted to bear. In retrospect his eagerness is not surprising, because he was a young Fleet Street two-guinea trifler called Pelham Grenville Wodehouse.

By 1923 (right) the ramparts of Bush House are rising, and the hoardings tell that at the London Palladium the American chanteuse Dora Goldberg, alias Nora Bayes, is holding court. Miss Bayes had become a star in the Ziegfeld Follies back in 1907, the year when, during the completion of the Kingsway

development (left), the billboard alongside the King's Tent was giving charitable instructions and the West London Mission was holding Sunday services at the Lyceum Theatre. Another aspect of show business is betrayed in the two men on ladders, making sure that everything that paste and water can do in the cause of Oxo and Company is being done.

THE GAIETY THEATRE in 1906. The milkman pushing his cart along the open road may or may not be aware that the Gaiety, its front entrance encumbered for the moment by a rubble-filled cart, is drawing the town with a musical comedy composed by Ivan Caryll (1861–1921) and Lionel Monckton (1800–1924). 'The Spring Chicken' opened in May 1905, so business must be steady.

By 1923, the proprietors of the theatre have begun to clutter the façade with electric lights. Caryll is dead and Monckton dying. But 'The Last Waltz', postwar though it might be (it opened in October 1922), would have fitted the Edwardian world like a glove, especially its music, composed by the relentlessly Edwardian Oscar Straus. Even the name of the lead-ing lady is venerable. Jose Collins was the daughter of the famous Lottie Collins (1866–1910), the music-hall singer who had drawn the town once upon a time with 'Ta-ra-ra-boom-de-ay!'

GAZING ACROSS Waterloo Bridge
from the Strand one day in 1923,
we peer in vain for some hint of the
far shore, or even for the faintest
rumour of a skyline. A year after
this photograph was taken, that
shrewd veteran Londoner H. M.
Tomlinson, finding himself confronted by the identical effect just
one bridge to the west, was
prompted to write: 'The bridge was
a shadow in the murk. It did not
cross the Thames. There was no
Thames. It was suspended in a void,
which it did not span; there was no
reason to cross because the other
side had gone. The bridge ended in
midway space.' And yet the scene
on this side is corporeal enough.
On the hoardings Oxo and Eno's
Fruit Salts stand alongside the
latest Hollywood sensation, 'The
Covered Wagon'. Someone is offering 'Government underwear', whatever that might be, at five shillings
a time, and even at this early stage
in the world's affairs Millet's Sur-
plus Stores are thriving. On the left
a lone policeman watches the man
crossing the road balancing baskets
of flowers on his head. The sheer
weight of traffic entering the West
End from the south side suggests
that it is morning and central London is still filling up in the course
of a routine working day. There is
a hole in the middle of the Strand,
but the men responsible for its administration are nowhere to be
seen. Perhaps they have gone off
for their mid-morning break to the
public house on the right.

THE SURVIVAL OF George Court far
into the twentieth century was a
persistent reproach to the planners
who had dreamed so long of widen-
ing the south side of the Strand
between Wellington Street and
Charing Cross Station. The most
mysterious thing about this 1923
glimpse of the Court is why it was
photographed at all. Whatever relevance George Court might have
had for the redevelopers, who saw
it as a stumbling block, or to those
two men gazing into a shop window,
who regarded it as a diversion, or
the man and woman weighing certain horticultural transactions soon
to be developed inside the station
and at the hospital on the south
side of the Strand, it was never going to be of much practical use to a
bus driver. It is characteristic of
White that he should nonetheless
have sensed the appeal of the moment and included it in a collection
where its irrelevance is comical.
Not all Londoners had the same per-
ceptions about the scenic charms of
George Court. As the camera clicks,
bowler-hatted, ultra-conventional
London strides ahead along the
Strand without even noticing the
brief access to the court, with its
touching invitation to see the
aviary.

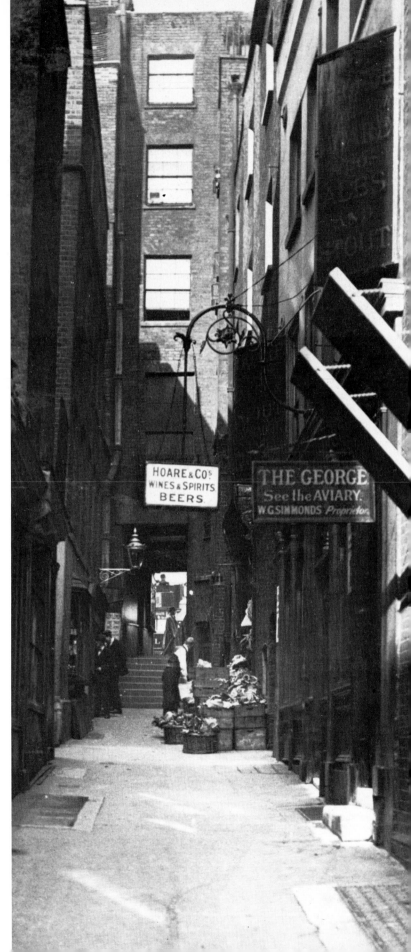

The pristine condition of the façade of the Tivoli Music Hall is explained by the fact that it is still only 1890 and the building has just been completed, on the site of the Tivoli Lager Beer Restaurant. One of the most spectacular of all theatres in the architectural sense, with Plantagenet windows, French Empire pilasters and a Romanesque attic, it is also one of the most expensive, costing £300,000, or roughly twice as much as its West End rivals. The Strand entrance is in fact the restaurant side, with the theatre behind. The ground floor buffet is in Indian style; there is a Palm Room, a Flemish Room and several private dining rooms. But this grandiloquence is about to be marred by two developments, the looming bankruptcy of its owners, and the fact that the architect, in his eagerness to create something beautiful, has forgotten to make it commercial, and overlooked the small detail that music halls generally do better business when they have a name. The lettering of 'Tivoli' here obscures the purity of that French Empire effect, and the line of its ground floor is destined always to be cluttered by posters. For all this, the Tivoli is about to become one of the world's most influential theatres. 'Tivolis,' says one historian, with no intention of punning, 'sprang up across the Empire.' It is destined to become the favourite London hall of men as disparate in spirit as the young

Surrey cricketer Jack Hobbs and the critic Max Beerbohm, who writes that, 'at the Tivoli most of the audience is prosperous.' In 1908, mounting a defence for the intellectual rigours of his play 'Getting Married', Bernard Shaw maintains that the disarray of the critics is due to the fact that he has written a good play and 'they are Tivoli critics'. Two years after this photograph was taken, the Tivoli, thriving under its new management, will advertise a programme of twenty-eight acts, including Eugene Stratton, Herbert Campbell and Bessie Bellwood, admission three shillings for stalls, two shillings in the pit, and a shilling in the upper circle.

On a day in the 1920s, with the Palace Theatre advertising the imminent return of Rudolph Rassendyll, one of the most spectacular structures in London stands sedately awaiting the end. The Hotel Cecil had opened in 1896 in a fever of magniloquent publicity – 'the biggest hotel on earth' – without any recorded comments from Jabez Balfour, the financier responsible for its conception, who shortly before the opening, found himself short of £8,000,000 or so, and was invited to spend the next fourteen years in a cell trying to remember where he had put it. If the Cecil was not quite the biggest hotel, it did have 1,000 rooms, each more splendid than the others, and, like a great many Victorian things,

came to enjoy a name for vulgar Edwardian ostentation. Its interior boasted multi-coloured marble; its corridors were lined with hand-wrought tapestries and decorated in what one pusher defined as Pompeiian style.

The Cecil was an anomaly, a giant whose great days had been at the turn of the century, when rich Americans flocked to it and foreign heads of state were received. It closed in February 1930 and was demolished in sixteen furious weeks to make way for Shell Mex House, leaving behind a faint bouquet of high life which perhaps survives a little in H. G. Wells' description of the Hardingham in *Tono Bungay*. All that now remains of Jabez Balfour's dream are a few overwritten brochures, scattered biographical references, and some sumptuous photographs to remind us that once upon a time people really did build hotels with 'Smoking Rooms in the Indian style'. As the bus conductor once said when the lady passenger asked him if he stopped at the Cecil, 'Wot, on twenty six shillings a week?'

THE STRAND CORNER HOUSE, with an unimpeded view down Craven Street to the distant Embankment. A sandwich-board man touts news of Bransby Williams at the Lyceum; nobody seems interested in the barmecidal feast on show in the Corner House windows. Inside, on floor after floor of beige-and-cream marbled halls, nippies dispense tea in heavy imitation silver pots, with strainers and milk jugs to match, chocolate eclairs and welsh rarebits, to a background of zigeuner music performed by kerchiefed bands of authentic gypsies recruited from the central branch of the Musicians' Union.

For once it is possible to name the very day of the photograph, thanks to the national Press. Outside the emporium of E. Whistler, Hammerless Ejection Breech Loaders, there stands a newspaper-seller whose placard reads: 'Dempsey Fight; Financial Fiasco'. Jack Dempsey, World Heavyweight champion since 1919, and destined to hold his position until sensationally outpointed by the Shavian Gene Tunney in 1926, was so charismatic a figure that only once was he touched by financial debacle. In the summer of 1923 he became involved in what he was later to define as 'the most fouled-up promotion of my life'. This fouling-up occurred in a no-horse town called Shelby, Montana, 'a crossroads in the middle of a desert', whose inhabitants had recently been galvanized by a small oil strike. A local panjandrum with a name straight out of Dashiel Hammett, Mr Foy Molumby, promised Dempsey $300,000 to fight an ageing journeyman called Tom Gibbons who agreed to fight for nothing. Only two-thirds of the purse was ever forthcoming, attempts to raise the balance failing because, as Dempsey put it, 'there wasn't that much money left in the town'. By July 3, the fight had been postponed six times. On July 4 it was called off a further seven times before at last commencing. Dempsey was taken the distance by Gibbons, after which he and his entourage ran straight from the ring to the Chicago train, leaving in their wake a maelstrom of bank failures and mortgage foreclosures. The news reached London on 5 July, 1923, when mid-day editions of the evening papers carried the story.

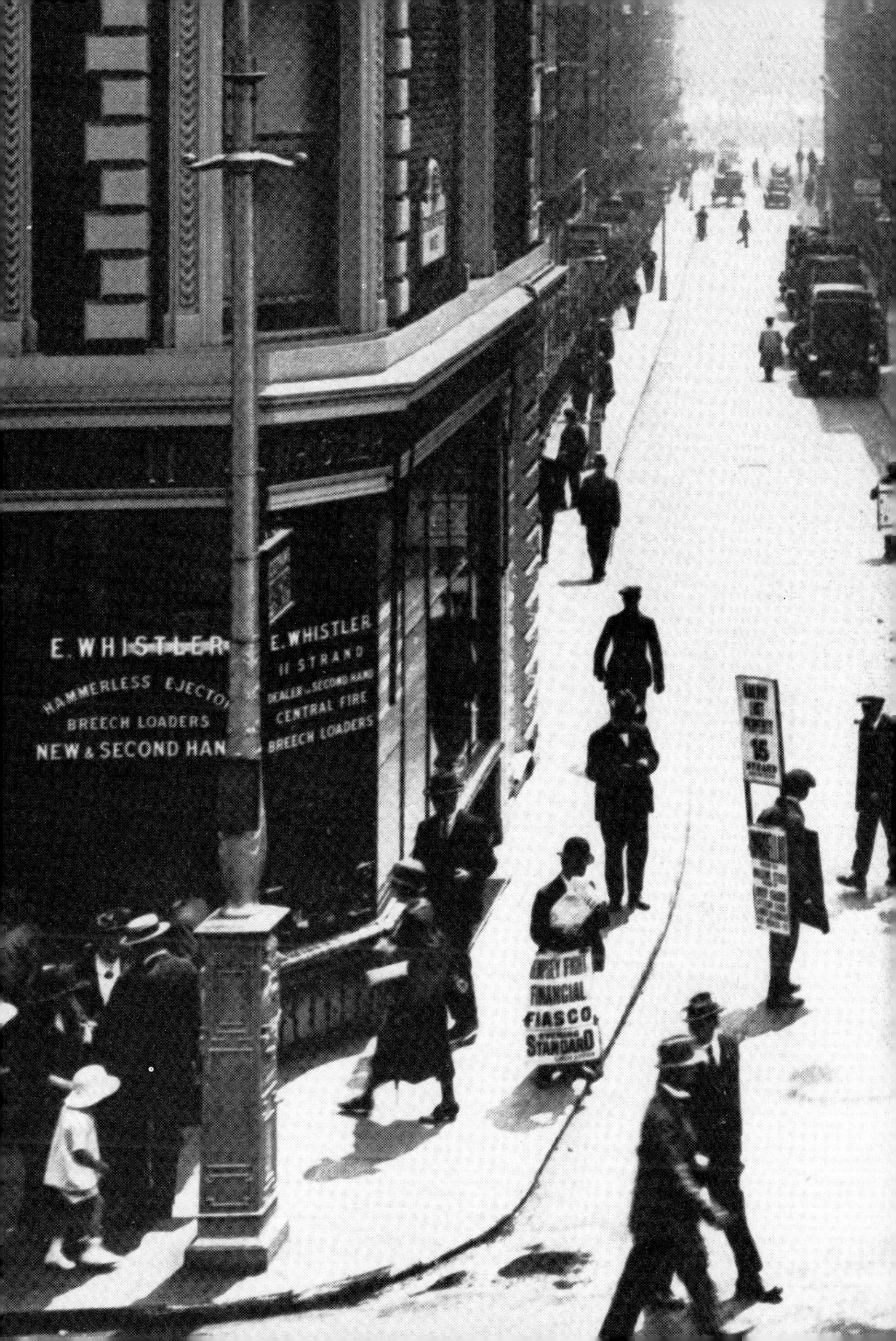

E. WHISTLER
HAMMERLESS EJECTO
BREECH LOADERS
NEW & SECOND HAN
E. WHISTLER
11 STRAND
DEALER IN SECOND HAND
CENTRAL FIRE
BREECH LOADERS
FINANCIAL
FIASCO
STANDARD
15

CHARING CROSS STATION in 1888, housing one of the great London hotels of the period. Traffic pours along the Strand, famous now as the street of hotels and theatres. The bus hoardings tell us that the Adelphi is persisting with its diet of melodrama – 'The Union Jack' – while at the Globe they are playing a farce destined to be remembered for the oddest of reasons. Even as this scene was being photographed, an England touring cricket side was flattening South African opposition under the captaincy of the Sussex player Smith. Soon after, Smith forsook green fields for green rooms and began an illustrious acting career in the title role of the 'Bootles' Baby' touring company. (He later explained, 'I played Bootles, not the baby'), from which moment he ceased to be known as Round-the-Corner Smith the eccentric bowler and was called instead C. Aubrey Smith of the hooded eyes and patrician profile. The station hotel has been a success from the start. Opened in 1865, a year after the station, it was half-full on its first night, and its Italian Renaissance interior, complete with 250 bedrooms, may well have been enhanced in the minds of prospective customers by the slightly gamey aura of the naughty continong which now attaches to the station, almost as though a whiff of bohemia has drifted across from the north side of the Strand, where the several small rooms of Romano's Restaurant provide a setting for discreet indiscretion. A. H. Binstead, chronicler of the less harmful dissipations of the town, writes:

The terminus of Charing Cross
Is haunted when it rains
By Nymphs, who there a
    shelter seek
And wait for mythic trains.

And John Betjeman, looking back to the Charing Cross of his boyhood as if to the promised land, was to be infinitely saddened by the thought that 'the shady ladies and young sparks to whom Charing Cross was the gateway to wickedness on the continent are dead and Charing Cross has become a commuter's station.' But not on this promising day in 1888, when the two policemen in the foreground may be waiting to question the old boy making such heavy weather of his descent down the curved staircase. The passenger on the upper deck of the 'Union Jack' bus is pointing at something with such urgency that he has attracted the attention of the driver sheltering under that superb umbrella. The stripes in the small of the driver's back may well confirm Frederick Willis's recollection that drivers in those days used to strap themselves in, a habit which, according to Willis, once gave a street urchin of his acquaintance the chance to jeer at a passing driver, "Oo strapped yer in, yer muvver?'

ALMOST HALF A century has passed, perhaps the most calamitous fifty years in English history. Charing Cross Station has surrendered its cosmopolitan reputation to Victoria, and a certain loss of identity is suggested by that lettering spread across the face of the station. Victorian Charing Cross would have regarded that kind of self-advertisement as superfluous, but now even the restaurant feels obliged to state its name, although that bulbous conservatory landmark at its eastern end remains intact. So do a surprising number of other things. The Bureau de Change and the continental tobacconists have both come through the Great War. The dispensing chemist in Villiers Street dispenses yet, and his neighbour who once advertised luncheons is providing the same fare but calling it refreshments. But the Criterion Outfitting Stores have fitted out their last. Considering all, Charing Cross is soldiering on rather well.

The street scene shows society struggling to meet the twentieth century but still vacillating between the horse and the internal combustion engine. Inside the hotel, the Victorian age lingers on; somewhere in its labyrinth there survives a Smoking Room, supervised by a white-coated waiter, who keeps an eye on the room's small library which includes full sets of Shakespeare and Scott. A century after the first photograph, fifty years on from the second, the Sherlock Holmes Society still holds its annual dinners at the hotel in deference to the topography of the canon. Something else has probably survived. The baby in arms in the foreground will be by now, with a modicum of luck, no more than venerable.

Looking into the station from the bridge, 1923 (inset). The station roof, a nondescript anticlimax after the rhetoric of the main building, is a mere afterthought, a legacy of the events of the afternoon of 5 December, 1905, when a hundred repair men on the station roof ran for their lives as seventy feet of the structure caved in, killing three of them. The side wall was pushed outwards on to the Avenue Theatre (now the Playhouse) in Craven Street, but the most ironic injuries were those sustained by members of the public. A few minutes before the catastrophe, three men entered one of the carriages of the 3.50 pm for Hastings in the reasonable expectation of arriving there. After all, there can be few safer or more peaceable pursuits known to an Englishman than catching the 3.50 pm to Hastings. Before their train left the station, the three men were crushed to death under a mountain of rubble. One pictures them meeting their maker while in the act of filling in *The Times* crossword or studying the latest news from the course in *The Sporting Life*.

82

CROSS
BUREAU CHANGE
Pears' SOAP
BRIGHTER LONDON
KEEP LEFT
GENERAL
GENERAL

LOOKING EAST ALONG the Strand
from the corner of Craven Street,
we see the London of 1923 hurrying
on its mercantile way, unconcerned
that in the last few years this street
has lost its reputation for being
the place for a man of the world,
for imperial adventurers home on
leave, for monied bachelors looking
for a night on the town. Three years
earlier A. G. Gardiner walked along
these very pavements and was so
touched by the cheeriness around
him that he declared, 'The Strand
to me is always the most attractive
street I know', and went on to suggest that he saw 'the wayfarers
transfigured into a procession
hurrying in pursuit of some sunlit
adventure of the soul'. In this scene
there is some evidence to support
him, even though Romano's restaurant is obscured by the mists on
the far northern side of the street.
Romano's, which somehow contrived to survive until 1948, was
founded by an Italian champion of
fractured English who boasted
proudly of the quality of his maca-
roni, received the accolade when
sketched by Phil May, and once, in
an attempt to win some money on
the horses, asked a tipster, 'What
win the Nateral Gland Bleeders
Coal Stakes?'

While there is nothing to match
Romano here, it is reassuring to
see that outside the ABC teashop a
bus conductor turns his back on
the timetables and chats with a
philosopher in a flat cap. Just behind them, leaning against a motor
car with left hand imperiously on
hip, stands a young woman whose
dangerous langour suggests some
unsung Iris March awaiting the
arrival of the partner who has
promised to meet her in time to
catch the boat-train from Charing
Cross. Or perhaps she is only that
girl in Wodehouse, 'with a laugh

like a troop of cavalry galloping
over a tin bridge', unaware that
even as she fumes, the bespatted
and homburged Wooster is picking
his way across the road towards
her.

'NELSON'S COLUMN TRAFALGAR DAY. 4632.
(1897.)

TRAFALGAR DAY 1897. The authorities, in deference to the sacred nature of the occasion, have patriotically recruited God as an Englishman, if the display at the foot of the plinth is anything to go by. Toppers mingle with boaters, bowlers with trilbies as the crowd, predominantly male, strolls past Landseer's avuncular lions. But mild-mannered London, accustomed to take for granted its own quiet affection for this most familiar of landmarks, would be amazed at the bitterness of Charles White's contempt. When it came to Trafalgar Square, White could hardly contain himself, apportioning the guilt in equal proportion to the government of the day which had impeded the architect Sir Charles Barry, and Lord Nelson, who, according to White, should not have been allowed in the Square at all: 'The proper treatment for the Nelson Column would be to remove the column itself to, say, the downs above Portsmouth, and to set up on the plinth a decent statue, more like Nelson than a Chelsea Pensioner.' Warming to his task, White decides that even this would be too good for such an architectural disaster: 'The whole Square might be shifted to Wanstead Flats or Wormwood Scrubs and Trafalgar Square remodelled on the lines of Barry's original design.' White's suggestions were never taken up.

TWENTY-SIX YEARS LATER the Square is almost empty (see overleaf). The church clock says five minutes past ten, as a lone ornithologist bends down to coax a resident on to his hand. A few yards away one man watches closely while another examines the soft underbelly of one of the lions, whose fellow, a few yards to the south-east, glares temerariously at the advertise-

ments of lurid tales of its homeland being displayed by the passing omnibuses. Another hero on whose behalf Charles White took up the cudgels was William Wilkins, who designed the National Gallery, or, as White puts it, 'tried to go ahead. The architect proposed. The Government disposed.' Soon White's rage has boiled over into capitals: 'The Gallery is marred, not by any shortcomings on the part of Wilkins, BUT BY DELIBERATE CUSSEDNESS ON THE PART OF THE GOVERNMENT OF HIS DAY AND THE SHORTSIGHTEDNESS OF MODERN ARCHITECTS.' Part of the trouble was the low elevation of the Gallery, which invited the overlooking intrusions of later developments. By the time this photograph was taken the interlopers had arrived, forcing White into even more typographical excess, which finally exploded in an exasperated scattering of dots and dashes: '. . . marred by unsightly structures erected by modern "architects"!'

THIS BEING AUGUST Bank Holiday, rain is falling, and it is just as well that the chaps climbing to the un-covered top deck have remembered to bring their caps along. As the queue patiently shuffles toward sanctuary, dreaming of the idyllic time to come in the Hampton Court Maze, the conductor stands watch-ing with a quietly proprietory air, holding behind his back the packs of multi-coloured tickets which one day will seem as sentimentally antique as the hemlines, the posters, and the bus itself. A few weeks earlier, on Whitsun Monday, 1923, the holiday travellers have been luckier with the weather. As they form ranks in Trafalgar Square awaiting the arrival of the bus that will carry them into the Green Belt and beyond, they carry their rain-coats over their arms and give the camera a festive smile, unconcerned by the presence among them of two men, the one in the military cap and his companion, who have either been lunching lately on H. G. Wells's food of the gods or are standing on orange boxes. But the celebrant who best expresses the exuberance of the occasion is the little girl striking a pose with such admirable unselfconscious-ness. And why not? It is bank hol-iday, the sun is shining, the hedge-rows beckon, and all is as right as can be expected in a world so con-gested with grown-ups. Sixty years later that young lady may be in-clined to take a modified view of things, and has almost certainly for-gotten that once, on a long-lost holi-day morning, flanked by parents who she can hardly remember now, she posed for posterity free of charge, and with such juvenile abandon as to embarrass the gentle-man behind her in the wing collar to look the other way.

THE OUTDOOR ORCHESTRAS of London vary in style from classicism to
anarchy and back again. A student
musician might be discovered pur-
veying Bach partitas on a venerable instrument in a shoe-shop
doorway. Squeezers of wheezy con-
certinas work the theatre queues
in nearby St Martin's Lane, and
the occasional veteran barrel or-
ganist rumbles the old favourites
on a machine festooned with views
of the Bay of Naples, and whose lid
is straddled by a red waistcoated
monkey, whose presence inspires
the wags to shout out requests that
he persuade his father to go away.
But the experienced London busker
is accustomed to genial abuse, and
is well able to counter it; when
asked by patrons if he plays by ear,
he will often reply, 'No, I usually
play around the corner'. Edwardian
Fleet Street was famous for a guitar-
violin duo who specialised in whimsical announcements of their programme, which usually included
Mendelssohn's Gin Song, Shool-
bred's Unfurnished Symphony or
one of Beethoven's Tomatoes. On
this morning, Whitsun 1922, the
pair working the Country bus queue
have more modest aspirations: a
capful of copper perhaps, for later
thirst-slaking. Most of the street
buskers you see these days display
the Mons Star, or carry a card
pinned to their jacket saying
'Blinded at the Somme'. Our duo
displays no hardware, and that
whistle contraption being featured
in the woodwind section seems less
an authentic musical instrument
than one of those ill winds that nobody blows any good.

RICHMOND

PICCADILLY
KNIGHTSBRIDGE
KENSINGTON ROAD
HAMMERSMITH BROADWAY
CASTELNAU BARNES COMMON
UPPER RICHMOND ROAD

THE
MIRROR
£10,000
BEAUTY
COMPETITION

THE
MIRROR
£10,000
BEAUTY
COMPETITION

33

THE RICHMOND OMNIBUS, crammed
with passengers, is just about to
begin its journey; the white-coated
driver is at the wheel and up on the
top deck the last traveller prepares
to take his seat. The weather is be-
nign, which is perhaps causing one
or two of the young ladies to harbour secret dreams connected with
that advertisement on the bus's
front. The *Daily Mirror* is holding
a beauty competition with a prize
of £1,000. That couple striding out
towards us, she in the black ensemble with the beads and hat, he
with bowtie and grey homburg at
snappy angle, look as though they
might be discussing what to do with
the winnings. Or is he merely beating time to the music of the buskers?
But the most striking thing about
this London holiday crowd is the
prevalence of the straw boater. Half
the men are wearing them; in the
story of the decline of male head-
gear, the extinction of the boater
except for purposes of fancy dress
will make a most affecting chapter.

Twenty minutes to four on an afternoon in 1923, and Charles White is moved to fulminate against the excrescences of the postwar world: 'Petrol, paint, sky signs and lavatories'. Bovril and Schweppes patiently await the onset of the dusk that will switch on their twinkling lights, at which point Charles I, up there on his stone horse, would probably attempt to emulate Leacock's knight and gallop off furiously in all directions if only to get away from Cromwell, frozen in stone a few yards down the road. A Great Western van trundles along at a pace so leisurely as to parody its own claims to 'express parcels and service'.

The entire scene is prosaic, from the English Speaking Union and the Chicago Daily News to Abdullah cigarettes and Randall's High-Class Boots – with the striking exception of the enigmatic figure in black, striding along with all the purposefulness of an Aldous Huxley heroine. Only one destination could possibly live up to her smart urgency, the marquee of the Grand Hotel across the road. A luxury hotel ideally equipped for assignations among the teacups, the Grand is at last drawing towards the end of its career. Four years later its owners will replace it with the Mayfair and convert it into offices, about whose walls will linger the ghosts of genteel adventurers who once sported in its Palm Court and Winter restaurant. In its heyday, up to 1914, the Grand had been a byword for Parisian chic, and the mysterious lady in black certainly seems up to the mark. Under that picture hat, are the eyebrows plucked, the hair bobbed? Is that handbag, so firmly clutched, capacious enough to hold one of those new-fangled long cigarette holders? And is her arrival eagerly awaited, or is that curtain, so discreetly pulled back on the third floor of the hotel directly above that awning a pure coincidence?

THE HIGH ROAD of the Empire, looking less like a high road than the main street of some wild west town. It is 1882. Mr Gladstone sits in Downing Street, although his home is in nearby Carlton House Terrace, a convenient location from which to conduct nocturnal operations involving the streetwalkers of the West End. Behind the façade of Horse Guards lies the parade ground, the largest clear space in London, it is said, except for the craniums of some of the men administering the great offices of state. In the streets the sombre tones of the clothing make a stark contrast with the quaint white-painted lamp-posts. On the eastern side, beyond the striped awning, lies the little court housing Cox's Bank, in whose vaults Dr Watson deposited the battered tin despatch-box containing records of untold Sherlockian adventures.

A few doors nearer occurs that bibulous arrangement by which Whitehall is, and will remain into the 1960s, the only street in London to boast three adjoining public houses. It is on their clamorous premises that, on nights of great Whitehall receptions, with the family coaches displaying emblazoned arms parked in the road, 'the horses out, the lamps shining', the coachmen and footmen moisten their throats and dispense intimate state secrets.

By 1923 the War Office has at last been promoted to Whitehall, and on that parade ground there now stand, fifty paces apart, those two deadly enemies, Wolseley and Roberts, resolutely not looking at each other. As they stare out towards the plains of St James's Park, perhaps they dream in their stony way of the good old days when Whitehall looked like the heart of a country town and the War Office

was a cluster of old private houses cunningly knocked together to resemble a labyrinth: 'It was all stairs and passages and landings, like some rambling old country house left behind in central London. There was the whiff of colza-oil lamps and leather fire-buckets; an office where private documents and public men could be lost without trace for weeks at a time.' But it is no longer of any importance. This is 1923, and the war to end wars has long since been fought and won, leaving workaday London to proceed on its pacifistic way.

IT IS A QUARTER past two on an afternoon in 1888. In Great George Street the hansoms clop down the century, the rhythm of their hooves soon to become identified with a new romantic hero who made his début last year in a book called *A Study in Scarlet*. But that was last season, the year of jubilee. The sensation of 1888 is a book of sketches of life on the far-flung outposts, entitled *Plain Tales from the Hills*. Here in Westminster, the posters proclaim a different kind of fireworks exhibition, one of Mr Brock's at the Crystal Palace. The following generation, being much less sure of itself, has dispensed with such frivolity, preferring the purlieus of government to be more august and much more boring. The ubiquitous Portland stone has reared its head again, lending to the arched access to new government offices a portentous echo of some imaginary ancient empire, Cicero, perhaps, in the Renaissance. Indeed, part of the southern tip of the street has been incorporated into Parliament Square in order that posterity may gaze on the edifying spectacle of statuary comprising Palmerston, Peel, Disraeli and Canning, the latter so overcome by an excess of analogy as to have attempted to pass himself off as an ancient Roman.

The skyline now is forbidding. The humanising hint of domesticity implicit in those first-floor balconies has been swept away, likewise that characteristic feature of Victorian London, the area railings giving on to subterranean kitchens whose scullions see life from the knees down, and whose narrow yards, cramped substitutes for front gardens, are a useful location for dustbins and dead sofas. None of the pedestrians gives a thought to the cellars of these houses, stretching out under the pavements. Fashions in dress in 1923 are duller but more comfortable, and much less stylised. That couple under the foliage of 1888, he frock-coated, she bustled and parasoled, are far too respectable ever to have heard of Georges Seurat, yet the accident of sunlight on sober suiting and black bombazine has created a silhouette which, discounting the monkey, is a witty echo of 'A Sunday Afternoon at the Grande Jatte'. But if you were to approach that upright Victorian couple and suggest to them that life sometimes imitates art – Seurat finished his painting two years ago – they would probably look away and call a policeman.

HUDSON'S SOAP
Sunlight Soap
HUDSON'S SOAP
SUNLIGHT SOAP
BEER
GINGER BEER

These
BUSINESS PREMISES
TO be LET
Apply
Messrs TROLLOPE
5, VICTORIA St s.w.
TO LET.
TO LET.
BEST PRICE
CLOTH

THE AUTHENTIC FACE of the working classes, sentimentalised in a thousand novels, apostrophised in a million pamphlets. This is the backstreet London celebrated by Hoxton's own, Marie Lloyd, who would have squirmed with delight at that flat cap sported by the matriarch with the shopping bag, and whose best-loved song concerned that bold economic stroke of the dispossessed, the moonlight flit. Here, on this grey morning in 1909, within hailing distance of Mr Asquith in his debating chamber, lives his electorate, in streets so blackened by absent-minded absentee landlordism that the very street-names are almost indecipherable. A board boasts of 'business premises for sale'. What business might that be, in a spot like this? A newsagent's specialising in *Dalton's Weekly*? Or a pawnshop perhaps, where they will advance you threepence for an old medal and ninepence for a wedding ring? The only creature-comfort in sight is the huge sus-

pended teardrop of the pub on the far corner, its façade blotted out by a stationary horse and cart. Charlie Chaplin, raised just over the water in Kennington, has stressed one blight of turn-of-the-century working class life, the lack of visual colour, which was a reality and not a retrospective trick of black-and-white photography. There certainly does seem to be a patina of soot lying across this whole scene. Even the black-and-white terrier looks black-and-grey. Were we to shake any of these adult hands, there would be grime under the knuckles, grime in the facial creases, grime in the wrinkles, grime in the crevices at the back of the neck, grime as all-pervading as the fog which permeates the opening paragraphs of *Bleak House*.

And yet White, justifiably repelled by the social injustices which the scene embodies, is overcome by that sentimental excess which often afflicts even the most dispassionate observer. He calls this scene

'Arcady in Westminster: The Eve of Departure'; any suspicion of irony is dispelled by his eager instruction: 'Observe the beauty of some of the children in the foreground.' But the man leaning with such studied mastery against the barrow, as though confident that his neckerchief is immaculately tied as befits a gentleman, would not thank White for the sentiment, is perhaps content with his lot, and would point to the rustic overtones of that pair of birdcages hung outside the window above as proof that life has its prettier moments even in Wood Street.

Looking down the same vista
from a vantage point further west,
we are on the threshold of Storey's
Gate, at the corner of Great George
Street. On the left is the old Insti-
tute of Civil Engineers; the first
floor window looking away from
Whitehall has the sunshade down
against the light of this spring day
in 1912. The low-lying three-storey
houses are an ironic comment on
the towers of government at the far
end of the street, but it is a comment
whose days are numbered. By 1923
the whole of the north side of the
street is given over to government
offices. No more are the lamps of
Storey's Gate presided over by the
livered beadle. And the cobblestones have gone, sacrificed to
macadam in the cause of smooth-
running bureaucracy. The Board of
Trade, the Ministry of Health, the
Education Department, all have
their files in triplicate in the area
now, and it is a truism that the
administration of trade, health and
education means foreclosing on
foliage and the eviction of the domestic spirit. In eleven short years,
sundered by the abyss of the Great
War, the street has been transmog-
rified from a place of human habi-
tation to a centre of power.

FEW LONDON THOROUGHFARES have ever undergone a metamorphosis more melodramatic than that experienced by Matthew Parker Street between 1904 and 1923. The later photograph, complete with gates of penal aspect and a gentleman wearing an overcoat with a velvet collar, shows the Wesleyan Central Hall standing on the right. Its presence here must constitute one of the most ribald juxtapositions in modern metropolitan history. Here, on the site of solemn piety once stood a famous Victorian folly called the Aquarium, one of the weightiest white elephants of its day. Its amenities included a winter garden, statuary, fountains, shrubs and empty seats, for it was capable of housing 2,500 people, few of whom ever turned up. When the building was formally opened in 1875 by the Duke of Edinburgh, it was claimed that in no other similar establishment in the world were so many different sights to be seen; presumably these included the Duke of Edinburgh. But the absence of paying customers caused the Aquarium to fall into decay, although its western end, housing the Imperial Theatre, enjoyed some sort of revival when taken over by one of the better actresses to come out of the Channel Islands, Lillie Langtry.

In the days before the rookery was swept away, those residents of Matthew Parker Street finicky enough to require the occasional draught of fresh air usually went out into the street to get it. There they stand one day in 1904, among the detritus of the imperial life, against a backdrop of barrows and parked perambulators, leaning against damp walls, standing in doorways, holding the baby in more senses than one, peering from upstairs windows at the occasional

stranger standing there on the
rough cobbles surveying the spectacle of life in the Royal Borough.
The paint peels off the walls, grilles
mark the awful blackness of basement rooms, rainwater festers in
the gutter. Matthew Parker Street
was only a few yards from and paral-
lel to Lewisham Street, and was
identical to it, being, in White's
words, 'a long, deep trench'.

LATTERDAY MILLBANK is an area so resplendently improved that almost nobody lives there any more, but earlier in the century the district comprised some of the most spectacular slums in London. They sprawled so generously that when at last they were cleared away an area of eight and a half acres had to be razed. The process was spread over so many years that it is impossible to put a precise date to the earlier scene, except to say that the photograph appears to have been taken on the very day that demolition began; perhaps that is why it was taken. At No. 69 it seems that, for the moment at least, a stay of execution has been granted. No lot number disfigures the brickwork, and the seagoing overtones of that splendid white-bearded veteran suggest that the Horseferry Wharf still conducts maritime operations. It is useful to note that according to the evidence the correct way to start knocking a building down is to dig up its doorstep.

Once the improvement is effected, we can stand in Abingdon Street and look south towards Lambeth Bridge confirmed in our suspicion that the world improves from day to day. Bankers and bureaucrats pad quietly along the western side, and the flags fly high over the soaring battlements of the new world.

Across the river the Archbishop sits in Lambeth Palace while the army of episcopal gardeners tend his herbacious borders. All seems to be well, but this is something of an illusion. Were we able to turn round and look in the opposite direction, we might feel nostalgic for those old slums. In 1950 Harold Clunn, tireless encyclopaedist of London, suggested that Abingdon Street was 'a magnificent specimen of real English ugliness'. Warming to his own revisionist form of demolition, Clunn goes on: 'Its appearance suggested the dustman sitting on the doorstep of the nobleman's mansion', and then impishly adds, as if in explanation of the general seediness of the scene, 'It was largely inhabited by Members of Parliament.' Lunn's use of the past tense is explained by the fact that Abingdon Street was badly mauled in the Blitz and subsequently rebuilt.

Clock Tower & Westminster Bridge

U1640

BETWEEN 1884 AND 1906, when these two photographs were taken, Time, if it has not quite stood still, has moved forward no more than ninety minutes. Very little seems to have changed, except that by 1891 the ramparts of Norman Shaw's New Scotland Yard were rising to dominate the northern approaches to the Bridge. By 1884 (above) Mr Gladstone has already committed the act which will eventually bring down his second administration, the despatch of General Gordon to the Sudan. But none of the travellers performing what the old sporting prints used to call the transpontine journey suspect the tragedy to come. Presiding over the later scene is Sir Henry Campbell-Bannerman, whose administration will long outlive him, and indeed itself also. The familiarity of this vista to the practised London eye obscures the fact that the scene is in fact two quite different scenes, with workaday London on the right and the fantastical vanities of mock-Gothic on the left. The bizarre architectural flourish of the Houses of Parliament, one of the very few buildings to achieve venerable status within minutes of being completed, probably shares with the red London omnibus the honour of being the best-known metropolitan symbol of all. Adjutants in dusty hill stations, postmasters in the veldt, boundary commissioners in Canada and Australia, all will pause occasionally, close their eyes against an alien landscape, and dream of these elfin towers, probably unaware that the flourish of lunacy attaches to their structure:

'The madman was Pugin, who covered the place with its immense Gothic detail inside and out down to the very inkstands and coat hangers. Pugin was Gothic mad. He was intoxicated by panelling, tracery and blank tracery, foliage, bays, emblems, oriel figures, turrets, and pinnacles. He was a marvellous and fertile artist of the kind who is easily broken by committees; he is said to have sketched in a fanatic uproar of story-telling and shouts of laughter. He was a devout Catholic. His end was to commit suicide at the age of forty, and there were dismal rows after his death, chiefly concerned with his share in the general design.' V. S. Pritchett; *London Perceived*.

WATERLOO PLACE, one of London's most popular dumping grounds for statuary, still retains in 1904 something of the feel of an open space dominated by the large memorial to the Crimean War, made from cannon captured at Sebastapol, and including at the back of the statue real mortars used in the battle. Other residents in bronze include John Lawrence, hero of the Indian Mutiny; Sir John Franklin, polar explorer; and Gentleman Johnny Burgoyne, spectacular loser in the American War of Independence.

By 1923 the place has become something of an inanimate rookery. Two years earlier the equestrian effigy of Edward VII galloped up only to find that earlier additions included Lady Scott's sculpture of her explorer husband; Florence Nightingale holding a lamp; Lord Herbert, the Minister for War who lent her support; and Sir Colin Campbell, who having been born the son of a Glasgow tradesman and now in danger of being outflanked by the motor car, is said by wags to have risen from the ranks only to become part of one.

Viewing the same scene from the Duke of York's Column, White begins to lose his temper: 'The Chief Commissioner of Police should make arrangements so that the King Edward statue stands alone, as a STATUE, not as a sort of mark for a car rank.' Of the view showing the same place from the north-east corner by Pall Mall, White rages on: 'Observe the disfiguring lamp standard and sand bin at rear of monument. Statues must be visible to traffic at night', which sounds like a hint that someone should have thought of lighting Miss Nightingale's lamp.

THE ATHENAEUM IN 1904, most prestigious of London clubs, those 'material monastries', as E. V. Lucas dubbed them, is the only one of its number to tolerate a female presence – the lady forever suspended over the portico is Pallas Athene. The club is noted for its impressive list of members, including J. M. Barrie and Henry James. Barrie is said by some to use the club as a writing room, but he will one day refute this, claiming that it was all he could do to reach the top of the entrance steps. It is James who provides the most telling glimpse of life inside the Athenaeum. In 1877 he describes a visit there, where Herbert Spencer is asleep – 'he always is whenever I come here' – the Archbishop of York 'has his nose in a little book', and the old boy in the far corner turns out to be a nephew of Lord Nelson; this James defines as 'the last word of a high civilisation'. He loved the Club: 'all the great chairs and lounges and sofas filled with men having afternoon tea – lolling back with their laps filled with magazines, journals, and fresh Mudie books, while amiable flunkies in knee-breeches present them the divinest salvers of tea and buttered toast.'

By the time that beautifully poised hansom turns towards the club entrance (previous page), James has removed himself to the more liberal Reform, club of Wells and Bennett, and has taken a room there high over Carlton Terrace – 'nothing could be more chic'. But here, too, Barrie has failed to convert himself into a good clubman, complaining that every time he goes to the Reform for a haircut, James is always sitting in the next chair having a shave. By 1923 James is dead and Barrie is still trying, but that chauffeur

reading his newspaper outside the
Carlton Club has probably skipped
the routine story of the misdemean-
ours of an English general and his
wife, and is scanning the stop press
columns for further news of the myr-
iad reasons why the Conservative
Party managers think less of Lord
Curzon than Lord Curzon does.
That shady character caught in the
act of entering the club is probably
one of those very managers.

Looking east along Pall Mall
from the vantage point of the old
War Office, 'that decrepit mauso-
leum', we can see, on this morning
in 1880, the ramparts of the Carlton
Club on the right – where else?
Next door is the Reform. The whole
area remains a male preserve, where
a gentleman can buy his wine, his
cigars, his uniforms, his boots and
his swords before beating a stra-
tegic retreat into his club.

THE REPUBLICAN MOVEMENT, its un-
crowned head bloody but still un-
bowed by the time this photograph
was taken in 1890, takes solace in
the thought that this palatial symbol of royalty is hollow in more
ways than one. Victoria, following
dutifully in the path of the Prince
Consort, has decided that London
is no place to live in, and once
widowed, shows a marked prefer-
ence for Windsor and especially
Balmoral, where John Brown
dances attendance whenever sober
enough. The monarch for whom the
palace had been built, George IV,
saw even less of it than Victoria.
Despite Nash's attempts to rush
the project through, the king died
before his home was ready to re-
ceive him. Parliament at the time
complained that the building was
'not plain enough', by which of
course it meant not cheap enough,
and one parliamentary aesthete,
contemplating its outline, described
it as 'a slop pail turned upside
down'. Victoria, then, may have
been justified after all in shunning
the place, a tactic so blatant that
in 1870 the Prince of Wales had re-
monstrated with her, saying, 'The
people do not like seeing Buckingham Palace always unoccupied', it
evidently never having occurred to
him that the people also did not
like seeing the Prince of Wales
always unoccupied. Both these
oversights were rectified once the
Queen was dead and the Prince
promoted to Edward VII.

By 1923 A SUCCESSION of reno-
vations have rendered the palace
more or less modern, with the old
queen commemorated in an item of
statuary placed before the front
face of the building. Most of her
old complaints have now been dealt
with, for in her day few of the lavatories were ventilated, there were
no sinks in the chambermaids' bedrooms, the bells refused to ring, the
doors refused to close, and the windows refused to open. Worst of all,
the building was ventilated through
the common sewer, and the drains
stank. Changes had come in 1901,
when the new king stayed at Marl-
borough House until the completion
of improvements, which included
the removal from the premises of
any evidence that John Brown had
ever been born. By 1907 the palace
was sumptuous enough to inspire
crowned heads to salivate; the
Dowager Empress of Russia declared, 'It makes one's mouth water
to see all this magnificence.' But
during her stay the Dowager Empress must have been reduced to a
degree of disarray spectacular even
for a Romanov, owing to the King's
psychologically intriguing habit of
tampering with the clocks. Having
been given to understand that punc-
tuality was the politeness of kings,
Edward had confused being punc-
tual with being premature and had
every clock on the premises set half
an hour fast, elevating the administration of the palace's social life
from dull reality to the wonderland
of the Mad Hatter's Tea Party.

In 1913 the building was given a
new façade in that standby of insti-
tutional London, Portland stone,
and the new processional road,
along which the royal gaze could
be directed from the palace bal-
cony, lined with young trees. But
on sunny days thoughts of royalty
were often eclipsed by the picture-
card prettiness of St James's Park
and the choreography of the ducks.
That archetypal Londoner leaning
on the barrier ponders problems
which must seem grave to him at
this moment. For his sake we hope
that that it is his bicycle waiting
on the other side of the road, and
that in a few moments from now
he will break up his tableau, take
to the saddle, and pedal sedately
home to an affectionate family in
Fulham or Islington or Enfield,
leaving the rest of the world to
gaze at what Eliza Doolittle, in the
years before her apotheosis, used
to call Bucknam Pellis.

ON AUGUST 30, 1905, the first Vanguard motor bus service to Brighton was inaugurated. It was an historic occasion and predictably the rubbernecks turned out with a proprietary air at Victoria to see the new service launched. The vehicle looks solid enough at first glance, but there were facets of its construction which must have made life extremely interesting for its pioneer passengers. In order to achieve the small turning axis so vital on London's congested roads, the designers had placed the back wheels perilously far forward, so that when approaching a stop while ascending a steep hill, under the weight of passengers crowding on to the stairs waiting to jump off the bus tipped up, in clumsy imitation of the rearing horses it had superseded. This eccentric alignment of the back wheels shows up clearly in the profile of a Vanguard in Trafalgar Square. 'Castles in Spain' dates the moment as 1906, and the foliage hints at late spring, which means that the bus would have disgorged most of its passengers at Lord's and Regent's Park Zoo. A few weeks before that first Vanguard motor-bus left for

Brighton, the last of the horse-drawn Brighton Mail Coaches had set out from Guy's Hospital. It was the night of Derby Day, and aboard to observe the passing of an age was the journalist James Bone, who recorded that after the team had been changed at Windsor and the coach cruised out into open country, 'our five noble lamps glimmered on the moving quarters of the horses and blanched the hedges.' By the time they reached the Downs the sun was up, and over the clopping of the team could be heard the piping of thrushes. 'Aged shepherds and cottagers hobbled to their doors, people waited at cross-roads, and early farmers drew up as the great red coach raced along the road for the last time.'

ON WHITSUN MONDAY 1922 (overleaf) a London crowd expresses its sense of joy by forming a queue at Victoria.

Judging from the appearance of those at the near end of the queue, Epping is about to be invaded by a contingent of Girl Guides. One man in a boater passes the time by reading a newspaper; just in front

of him an observant woman looks incuriously at us; a few paces behind a young mother stands a little apart from the queue and cuddles her baby. That spirit of cautious optimism which typifies the town is perfectly expressed by the couple walking towards us. The lady holds onto her partner with one arm; in the other she carries a topcoat. There seems to be a general feeling of good humour abroad in the air, and yet according to the essayist Robert Lynd, a man addicted to bus rides: 'If gaol were anything like the inside of a motor bus with standing room for five only, no man who was not either mad or a born criminal, would risk committing any offence likely to send him there. I can think of no more effective kind of prison reform than to abolish the prisons and commit criminals to the insides of motor buses instead.' Lynd expressed these sentiments in the same year that this happy photograph was taken.

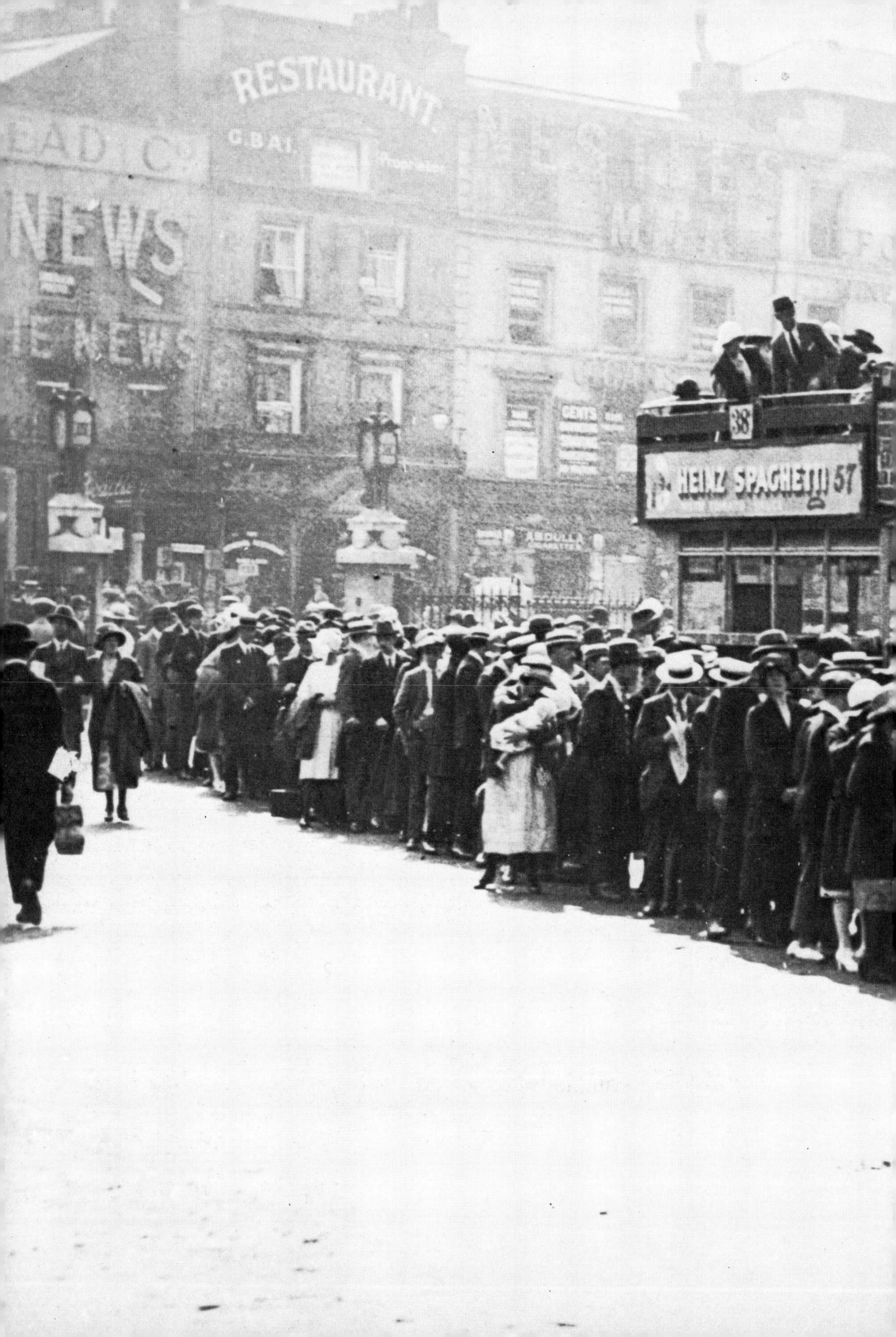
RESTAURANT
NEWS
GENTS
38
HEINZ SPAGHETTI 57
ABDULLA

THE SOUTH-WEST CORNER of Sloane Square in 1895. Throughout the decade demolition and redevelopment has been proceeding at a furious pace, confirming the integration of the old village of Chelsea into western London proper. The Royal Court Theatre has been here since 1871, and the plane trees of the Square, part of whose foliage just obtrudes into the right foreground, are mere saplings no longer. But the Royal Court Hotel will not open its doors until later this year, and the lot numbers daubed on the shop-fronts are a telltale indication that soon there will be further flattenings. In the centre foreground a passer-by with gleaming white wing collar stands with hands in pockets, and, if he is one of the intellectuals for which the area is notorious, is perhaps savouring one of the most ridiculous accidental puns that the streets of London have ever offered. That clock dominating the upper floors of Sir Thos. Dodd and Co., Glass Shades, with the letters of 'The Pottery' instead of numerals, has stopped once and for all at twenty five minutes to six. With demolition imminent, its active life is clearly over, a condition graphically spelt out by the description 'No Tick' which looms above it.

RAILWAY.
CITY
WEST END, &C.
SLOANE SQ STATION
TO BOOKING OFFICE & TRAINS
DISPENSARY
BY
CONTRIBUTIONS.
FUNDS
BUILDING OF
NEW PREMISES
MANOR ST CHELSEA

SLOANE SQUARE, the eastern end of the south side in 1895. Despite its air of a sick animal, the dispensary will not be demolished for another five years yet, so perhaps the desperation of that notice between the ground floor windows exaggerates the crisis just a fraction: 'Funds are urgently needed', it cries, 'for the building of new premises.' In the meantime it appears to be supported, not just by voluntary contributions but also by timber stays whose exposed flank features a hoarding proclaiming the primacy of Cerebos Salt. Among the other casualties of imminent development is the dispensary's next-door neighbour, the scholastic agency which modestly describes itself as 'high-class', although its pretensions are compromised more than somewhat by the board offering houses, flats and stables. In these days London is scattered with establishments of this kind which, if H. G. Wells is to be believed, specialise in the placing of intellectual square pegs in loosely educational round holes. It is in just such an agency as this that young Mr Lewisham learns that for all his youthful agnosticism, he will have to teach religion; on complaining he is told, 'That's nonsense. You can't have everything, you know.' And when his subsequent answers to the agency's questionnaire seem doubtful, he is advised that should he fail, then there is nothing left but the lower depths, 'Journalism or the London Docks'.

By 1923 the dispensary and the scholastic agency are a fast-fading memory. A block of flats serves as their headstone, and a bank and a bookshop are among the ground-floor usurpers; it is a balmy day, judging from those open windows on the second and third-floor flats above the bank. But one day this

peaceful backwater will be disturbed by something a little more alarming than the dialogue at the theatre adjoining the railway station. Sloane Square booking office stands with a fine modernistic flourish which will be flattened when a bomb falls on it seventeen years later.

IN THIS 1923 SCENE of Kensington High Street, showing the western extension of Derry and Toms and the rebuilt underground station, the world seems thoroughly urban, thoroughly modernized. Commerce chugs along. Jaeger jostles the ABC tea-rooms, and Walpole Brothers are holding a linen sale. Yet not so far away, backwaters remain. In Cheyne Walk, looking east from Cheyne Row (left), a small-town hush is evoked by the unattended milk cart; in the far distance the hazy rumour of approaching pedestrians, but otherwise no sign of life. But it is an illusion after all. By 1923 Chelsea has long since surrendered any lingering pretensions to descent from the Victorian village that was so loved by Thomas Carlyle and Leigh Hunt.

In the glimpse of the western end of Cheyne Walk in 1888, there must be several people who remember Hunt, who came here and spoke of being 'embalmed in silence'; Carlyle, who lived out his life at No. 5 (now 24) Cheyne Row, and grumbled at the absence of hills; John Stuart Mill, who kept Carlyle company on his walks about the area; George Eliot, who moved here in 1880 hoping that Chelsea's mild air would improve her health and died nineteen days later; Dante Gabriel Rossetti, who followed her in 1882 after having devoted so many years to a calamitous attempt to create a bestiary at Tudor House, and whose peacocks rehearsed their eldritch cry so persistently that forever after the Cheyne Walk leases included a clause forbidding the birds on the premises; Oscar Wilde, who used to place a Persian screen before his smoking-room window to blot out the sight of the slums of Paradise Row. The policemen in particular might have cause to re-call young Mr Swinburne, who in warm weather would take all his clothes off and leap around Tudor House with a lack of self-consciousness amounting to sheer frenzy. Already the farms and the fields and the market gardens have gone, along with the foreshore, buried under the headstone of the Embankment in 1874. In the old days at Tudor House, the river would lap into Rossetti's cellar at high tide. But now the old skylines that Whistler had so diligently trained himself to memorise, are fast disappearing. Even the public house, which boasts of having been established more than a century ago, is advertising a mixture of 'soda and milk'. Whatever would Mr Swinburne have said?

WE ARE IN KNIGHTSBRIDGE, looking east from Albert Gate. The year is 1885. That cluster of parasols and toppers in the left foreground, the half-lady walking away from us and the half-horse emerging from a side street, the man about to enter on transactions with the juvenile street trader, all of them have that self-conscious look of having been rehearsed in their positions. Elsewhere the photograph flows more informally. The immaculately accoutred coachman drives his mistress dutifully west, while behind him on the corner thrives the Albert Gate offices of the Great Northern Railway, whose sign seems to be performing a multiplicity of purposes, advertising not only railway tickets, dentists and *The Daily Telegraph* but also the availability of diamonds, pearls, plate and jewels. The only pedestrian who looks opulent enough to consider the diamonds is that splendidly white-whiskered patriarch accompanied by the lady in black. What are they discussing, this earnest couple performing their Trollopean duet. Perhaps the quality of

the new best-seller, *King Solomon's Mines*. Or the chances of survival for the new Savoy opera, 'The Mikado'. Or perhaps even the new publication, *The Dictionary of National Biography* and whether white-whiskers has any chance of ending up in its pages.

Forty years on. How has the town improved itself? The church with its proud spire has been conjured away, like all its parishioners; indeed that whole side of the street has gone, including the premises of the clamorously named Mr Shout the jeweller, clearly an associate of Mr Bun the Baker. The welcome flourish of rusticity provided by the trees has all but vanished. The horses are gone and with them their generous contributions of droppings. The borough has improved the street lighting, and now two policemen are in evidence; one of them seems anxious to apprehend somebody for a traffic offence, while the other gazes wistfully after the Hornsey Rise omnibus. The bus travelling the other way features a conductor collecting fares on the upper deck. 'Don't forget your

Home and Colonial Tea', says that No. 73 bus for Roehampton, and then adds as an afterthought the news of Schweppes' Mineral Waters and the imminence of the marriage of the Duke of York to Lady Elizabeth Bowes-Lyon. It is a plainer world which has replaced the old one, a world less disposed to fancy dress and with much less reason for wearing it.

THE RING, HYDE PARK, 1885, looking north-east to the battlements
of Park Lane. We are near the
Achilles statue erected in 1822 by a
mysterious body calling itself 'the
women of England'. It is difficult to
decide which was the more ludi-
crously named, the group or the
statue, which has nothing to do
with Achilles, being a copy of an
ancient figure of a horse-tamer on
the Monte Cavallo in Rome. This
section of the Park has been the
scene of fashionable promenades
since the time of Charles II, and by
now is approaching its zenith. The
riot of victorias and landaus, livery and cockades, reminds us that
this is the milieu of the Forsytes,
whose most horsey representative,
Swithin, takes great pains to deck
himself in frock-coat, doe-skin
gloves and bell-shaped topper before
exhibiting himself with his four-in-
hand. Elsewhere Galsworthy writes
that at this time of year 'the Park
and all sweet-blooded mortals in it
nod and smile.' He does not go into
details as to what it is they are nod-
ding and smiling at; to do so would
be thought as indecorous as drawing attention to that lone obtrusive
specimen of dung in the left foreground of the photograph. But the
fashionable parade is not quite
as starchy as its leaders of fashion
would have us believe. In 1861,
Catherine 'Skittles' Walters, mistress of many arts and a great many
well-appointed men, and an excep-
tional horsewoman, was hired by a
Berkeley Square livery stable to
advertise their horses by driving a
phaeton along the Ring. Her impact
on society was devastating, as her
employers had been thoughtful
enough to equip her with a riding
habit which was, in the words of
L. C. B. Seaman, 'so closely moulded
to her figure that it had to be worn
next to her skin.'

THE ARRIVAL OF THE motor car has endowed the streets of London with a property unknown in the days of the horse-and-carriage – what might be called dateability – the existence of clues to put a year to the moment. Charles White has marked down the scene on the previous page as 1923, and yet the hardware in evidence would seem to contradict him. The Rolls Royce Silver Cloud is, it is true, an early 1920s model, and sports a feature which makes a revealing comment on niceties of class distinction. Above its wooden wheels it has an open front, that is to say, although it has a windscreen, they are accompanied by no side windows. This style soon became obsolete with the acknowledgement that even the most obsequious and deferential chauffeur required a little protection from the winds of fortune.

The other car in the foreground is a Gwynne 8, manufactured by a company which will survive as Gwynne Pumps Limited: its number-plate is what betrays White's error. The registration indicates late 1924 or early 1925. Even wider of the mark is that Citroen to the left of the other two cars, a model which was not launched until 1927. Connoisseurs will pick up at least two other features of the scene; the presence of a Buick which, when added to the evidence of the Citroen, suggests that even in these imperial days, the motor car industry is prone to assaults by importers, and second, that concern for any sort of Highway Code is still a purely personal affair, otherwise how do we explain the prevalence of so many U-turns on this major road?

ONCE UPON A TIME the phrase 'The Season' had been evocative of an elite parading itself, free of charge, for the instruction of the lower orders and the edification of fashion editors and society columnists. Hyde Park, and especially Rotten Row, is the venue for the execution of this nebulous tribal dance, but by the semi-mechanised 1920s, much of the exclusivity and all the elegance has gone, mislaid somewhere on Flanders Fields. The style of the old season had depended for the most part less on gentility than on dressmakers, and had been distinguished by the breeding, not of its heroes and heroines, but of the horses that pulled them. But by 1923 the equipages and the liveried servants have all gone, to be replaced by motor cars which are already beginning to roof themselves in with weatherproof anonymity.

THIS SHOT OF THE Screen at Hyde Park Corner on the north side of Piccadilly, taken in 1903, gave White a welcome chance to pour derision on his betters. Decimus Burton (1800–81) was one of White's architectural heroes, which is not surprising considering that he designed the Colosseum in Albany Street, the gardens of the Zoological Society, the Athenaeum Club and much of the building at Kew Gardens. When it came to the Screen, however, he ran into trouble with the authorities. Burton's idea was a Roman arch embellished with bas-relief sculptures and surmounted by a quadriga. But there was already in existence at Apsley House a ridiculous equestrian effigy of the Duke of Wellington, and it was this object that the powers selected to crown Burton's arch. Unfortunately in this statue the Duke is depicted in a top hat, and as top hats had not been conspicuous at the time of the Roman Empire, Burton was understandably embarrassed that the symmetry of his concept should be ruined in this

lunatic way. White goes on: 'Burton was helpless, and so greatly did he feel and resent the misuse of his fine arch that he made a clause in his will providing the nation with the sum of £20,000 to cover the expense of moving the Duke's monument. This clause Burton cancelled before he died. Although he did not live to see the removal of the mon-

strosity, he survived long enough to know that arrangements to this end had taken tangible form, in the shape of the Hyde Park Improvement, which was carried out a few years after his death.' The problem of the Duke's top-hatted statue was to cause much trouble over the years. Having been moved from Apsley House to the Screen, it then

galloped to the top of Constitution Hill, but even this was not thought far enough, and the riddle was not finally resolved until it was removed to Aldershot and beyond the limits of this volume.

139

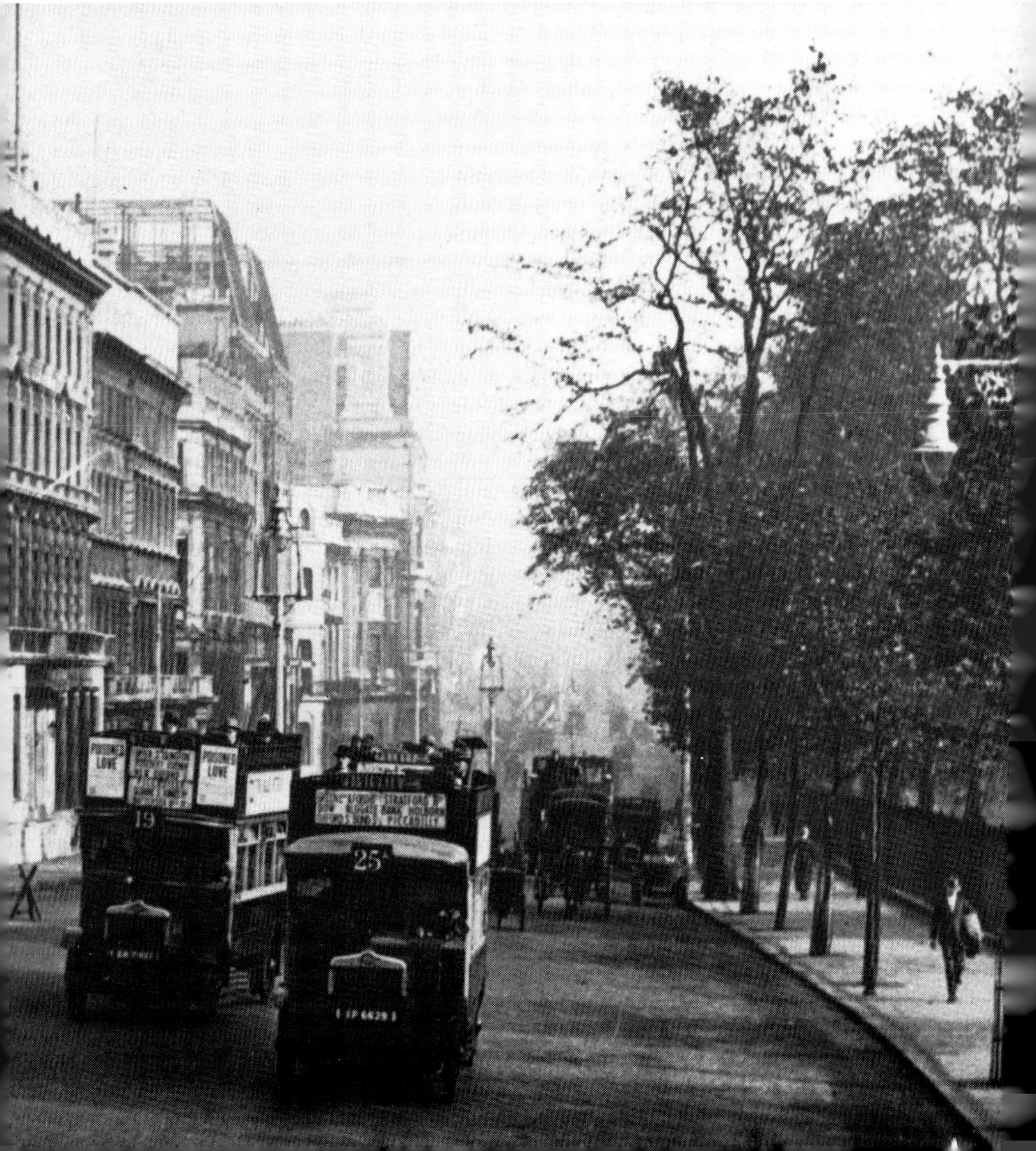
LOVE
LOVE
19
STRATFORD
PICCADILLY
25A

THERE IS SOMETHING a shade too impersonal about the stone face of Piccadilly as it looks out across the plains of Green Park. As a thoroughfare it remains fashionable enough, but it appears to have forfeited much of its old domestic aura. A generation earlier, on the site of one of these vast stone terraced palaces, there had stood the house of Baroness Burdett-Coutts which Queen Victoria had so enjoyed visiting. It had been the royal pleasure to sit at an upstairs window watching the traffic go by, but on this bright Georgian morning the only traffic consists of two of White's homely leviathans apparently having a race along Piccadilly, with the No. 25 half a length in front of the No. 19, no doubt borne down by the dead weight of the item it advertises, 'Poisoned Love'. This may well qualify as the oddest piece of publicity in the entire White collec-

tion, and also perhaps the most alarming. Frederick Willis was not the first Londoner to point out the danger that unsophisticated or shortsighted passengers might well prove incapable of distinguishing advertising from editorial matter: 'Buses were embellished with various cryptic signs which must have been very confusing to the stranger. "Bank, Bovril, Somerset House, Hudson's Soap, Trafalgar Square and Vinolia" were blended into a fascinating but bewildering combination so that a foreigner could hardly tell whether Piccadilly was a patent medicine or Pink Pills a place of destination.'

But there are always the inimitable milestones to guide the waifs and strays. The Ritz Hotel, symbol of a vanished chic, stands as firm as any of the French chateaux it was designed to emulate. It opened in 1906, the first large-scale steel structure in London; for months

before it was completed, the passerby could see the steel ribs open to the elements before that elegant stone overcoat was moved into place. The omnibus heading our way is just abreast of that delightful covered promenade, half-hotel, half-pavement, which lends a *soigné* Parisian air of romance to the occasion. Monsieur Ritz was a restaurateur who became immortal for having fed so sumptuously those Londoners able to afford it. Perhaps that sweetbread importer is even now clopping to the Tradesman's Entrance with fresh consignments of delicacies.

U1646

PICCADILLY IN 1923, with a commissionaire gazing vigilantly westward from the threshold of Fortnum and Mason. Two taxi drivers stand at the head of the rank in the middle of the road, idly passing the time of day; one of them scratches his head in perplexity; perhaps he has just heard news of the Dempsey–Gibbons fight (see photograph on page 78). A van-boy, decapitated by a shadowed interior, stands on the edge of his cart, the stance of his legs echoed beneath by the plodding hooves of the horse. The Bluebird Restaurant demonstrates the extent to which fashions change. Fifty years before the ooze of musak and the blast of the discothèque, its banner proudly boasts the absence of music as one of its prime virtues. Had the cameraman stepped back a yard or two, we might have seen the gated Piccadilly entrance to Burlington Arcade, complete with the beadle so fulsomely celebrated by Dickens and Gilbert, and whose duties include the prevention of whistling and the proscribing of perambulators. Only one person in the photograph suspects our presence, and she is so far removed from the scene that not even the photographer is aware of her. High above the musicless Bluebird, in a glass-walled eyrie commanding a view of the whole of Piccadilly, there stands a young woman peering through the panes. Like the skivvy at the razing of Newgate, she is rendered ineffably mysterious, by her remoteness, her anonymity, her idle curiosity.

presenting more than one attraction at a time, a fact which proved to be the undoing of poor Benjamin Robert Haydon, the painter who staged an exhibition of his own work there in 1832, only to watch the whole town pass him by and crowd into the other entrance to see General Tom Thumb. Mortified by the experience of being upstaged by a midget, Haydon rolled up his canvases, vacated the Egyptian Hall, and went home to blow his brains out.

Among the forgotten lions who once triumphed at the Egyptian Hall were the lecturers Albert Smith and Artemus Ward, and, much later, The New English Art Club as represented by the work of Wilson Steer, Sargent, Augustus John and Rothenstein. But the man who raised the Egyptian Hall to its pinnacle of fame was the great illusionist John Nevil Maskelyne. In harness with his partner George Cooke, Maskelyne pioneered the art of stage magic; in 1871 the Reverend Dodgson, overcoming his distaste for theatrical frivolity by metamorphosing into Lewis Carroll, returned to the hall once more, this time not to see the Israelites advancing on Jerusalem but to witness the brilliant prestidigitations of Maskelyne. As the age drew to its close, Maskelyne became more and more closely associated with the Hall, and the Hall with the art of making its next trick seem impossible. James Bone said of its demolition: 'It vanished with its stucco monoliths and gods and goddesses like one of the acts of those great illusionists and a huge stone building appeared in its place.'

THE EGYPTIAN HALL, 170–1 Piccadilly, on a day in 1905, poised on the brink of demolition. One of the town's most popular commercial galleries, it had opened in 1812, the first public building in London to be designed in mock-Egyptian style, its façade supposedly in the form of an ancient Egyptian temple. To the modern eye it looks modest enough, but the sphinxes over the entrance and the stucco monoliths of the gods dominating the threshold must have shone with an exotic light in the midst of all that Georgian architectural respectability. The hall was used for a bewildering variety of entertainments, from paintings to the Diorama showing the advance of the Israelites from the Land of Goshen to Jerusalem which evoked the admiration of the Reverend Dodgson when he witnessed it in 1851. But the hall was capable of

IT IS 1895, as we look north-east down Shaftesbury Avenue. At Westminster my Lords Rosebery and Salisbury are gravely exchanging the parliamentary baton. In this year three harbingers of the future, none of them British, makes three giant strides. The harbingers are Marconi, Lumiere and Rontgen, the strides Wireless Telegraphy, the Cinematograph and the X-ray. Meanwhile a flag whickers bravely over the battlements of the London Pavilion, and a human hoarding trudges the gutter in the cause of Charles Hawtrey in 'The Private Secretary' at the Avenue, a theatre destined in ten years from now to fall over when part of the roof of Charing Cross Station caves in. Only one man in this scene has grasped the proposition that immortality, behind the camera shutter, is staring at him. And he, resplendent in bowler, intaglio ring and buttonhole, stares back. Probably he bought the flower a few moments ago from one of 'The Girls' behind him. These flower-sellers are among the most famous of all metropolitan landmarks, but one day they will go the way of the Avenue Theatre and all their customers, destined to survive only as the legendary heroines of a celebrated Crazy Gang sketch. A generation later a journalist will report a conversation with one of them reminiscing about the 1890s: 'In the old days every kebbie had his buttonhole, and no gentleman was dressed unless he had one too. And the drivers of the old horse omnibuses! They were rare customers – nice, pleasant men, too, who liked to pass the time of day with you and talk. Now there's no time for talk or flowers.'

IN 1893 THE GENTLE curve of Nash's Regent Street remains unbroken, the perfect symmetry of its arc endowed with a humanising whimsicality by the irregular ranks of chimney pots stretching away towards Regent's Park, Hampstead and infinity. The militant lady on the County Fire Office roof has a faintly portentous air, but all else retains a domestic proportion modest enough to be dominated by one of Charles White's special favourities among the statues of London. Alfred Gilbert's memorial to the Earl of Shaftesbury shows Eros frozen in the act of firing an arrow at Mr S. Van Raalte cowering invisibly behind the windows of the family cigar shop. But the intended symbolism designed by Gilbert was, according to White, to show our hero 'discharging the arrow of love and charity, unmindful of the insecurity of foothold and striving only to reach humanity with his shaft.'

Throughout the twentieth century the British, confronted by the bold challenge of this open space, will bungle and vacillate, remove poor Eros and put him back again, rearrange the buildings in such a way that a more appropriate name would be Piccadilly Square, and generally show an irresponsibility regarding the Circus's amenities amounting to moral imbecility. Nobody in this photograph dimly suspects that his grandchildren will live to see the area reduced to the status of slum and eyesore, while Gilbert's fine statue, the one which according to White so delights the aesthetic soul of Japanese tourists, will endure such indignities that it will at last become the ambition of every celebrant Londoner, in the words of V. S. Pritchett, 'to climb the statue of Eros, and, preferably, damage it.'

A NEW GENERATION has arrived, bringing with it the disruptive elegance of the Piccadilly Hotel. The lady on the Fire Office Roof stands firm, as though confident that when, in three years time the building is redesigned in more spectacular style, she will retain her lofty eminence. A few yards to the north, extensive building operations proclaim themselves with steel girders pointing to the sky. There has been a shower; a few umbrellas are still up, and both the policeman on point duty and the coach driver still sport their waterproofs. But the rest of London seems happy to come out of its shell, evidently undistressed at the spectacular decline in lamp-post design. Three years after this moment, that quaint survival on the north-west corner will be swept away by the inexorable advance of Messrs Swan and Edgar. But that will not be until 1926. In spite of the justified fulminations of Charles White – 'lack of foresight displayed by the authorities', 'Great Windmill Street should have been widened', 'the Circus should have been laid out more on the lines of a square', 'generally congested owing to carts unloading goods at the Trocadero' – despite all this, the Circus remains a residue of affectionate recollection. Even Henry James, whose fastidiousness ran riot when he complained of 'the uproar' of Piccadilly and 'the rattle of a heartless hansom as it passed close to my ears', recalled with some warmth that it was from The White Horse, buried today in the underground station, that all coaches would start their journeys, and that on Derby Day, when all were Epsombound, there was a general prevalance of hampers and champagne.

In 1881, THE NORTH side of the eastern end of Piccadilly Circus houses a London Pavilion unrecogniseable as the grandiose theatre of later years. This early Pavilion had begun as a stable yard, acquired a roof when some showmen exhibited waxworks there, then became a skating rink, and finally a theatre of sorts. It was well placed for all its modesty, because in 1881 the Music Hall was poised on the threshold of its golden age. In 1885 the new Pavilion was to open, but purists would wonder if the entertainment was any better than the rough-and-ready bills of the old days. On this day in 1881, while the tradesmen, the onlookers, the bearded policeman and the carthorse show varying degrees of interest, the one-time stableyard offers famous names. James Fawn is an actor-singer whose reputation will prove less enduring than his repertoire; his big song is 'If You Want to Know the Time Ask a Policeman'. Fred Albert writes all his own songs. G. H. Macdermott does not, but in 1877 he gave the language a new word when he sang 'We Don't Want to Fight But By Jingo if We Do'.

The biggest attraction of all is Bessie Bellwood, the stage name of Kathleen Mahoney, an East End rabbit puller who took to the ribaldries of the emergent music hall as though born to them. One of the first female stars, she is one of the most extraordinary characters of her day, her London début at the Star, Bermondsey being so riotous that it was reported in detail by Jerome K. Jerome. Faced by a rowdy mob led by a coal-heaver, Miss Bellwood abused her persecutor for five and three quarter minutes without pause: 'At the end she gathered herself for one supreme effort, and hurled at him an insult so bitter with scorn, so sharp with insight into his career and character, so heavy with prophetic curse, that strong men held their breath while it passed over them, and women hid their faces and shivered. Then she folded her arms and stood silent, and the house, from floor to ceiling, rose and cheered her until there was no more breath left in its lungs.' She composed her most famous song, 'What Cheer 'Ria', but a better idea of her virtuosity may be gathered from the fact that once, within four hours of a conversation with Cardinal Manning about some Catholic charity, she was arrested for knocking a cabman down in Tottenham Court for attempting to insult her. She died in 1896 at the age of thirty nine, burnt out by what her biographers chivalrously define as a bohemian existence.

By 1923 the only live bodies left in the rebuilt Pavilion are the ones in the seats. The silver screen has replaced the old music hall stage, and an American impersonator of Robin Hood vies with Veno's Cough Cure for the attention of the people milling about among the cars and horses.

IF THE FAÇADES of late Victorian Regent Street seem the last word in bleached perfection, that is because the leaseholders are obliged to repaint their stucco at least once every year. Regent Street is a promenade for the Olympians. Queen Victoria's hatters, Messrs Johnson and Co., would be easy enough to find if you could borrow young Mr Wells' time machine and wander into infinity down the right-hand side of the road. You can buy everything here from mourning clothes to three hundred guinea Cashmere shawls. An aristocracy sadly afflicted with mortality comes here to purchase its urns and obelisks, its stone angels and broken columns. But it also buys clotted cream, tapestries, flowers, paintings, perfume, millinery, lace, furs, wine, liqueurs and caviar. In this street the Duke of Wellington's bootmaker lives on, and just round the corner, in Albany, that felonious master of the leg-break, A. J. Raffles, ponders the problem of how to relieve establishments like Shepheard and Reed of their stocks. If that shop is too modest, then there is always the grander house of Charles Packer, which, on this day in 1886 is, judging from the 'Mourning' ads, hoping for a few deaths in the family. Life, however, to say nothing of commerce, is for the living, and while the sandwich-boards proclaim the primacy of Salutaris Mineral Water, a young man contributes further to the elegance of Regent Street by gathering manure. Clearly his is the least rewarding occupation on view, because he alone has stopped working in order to study the camera.

THIS PHOTOGRAPH OF Regent Street in 1907 is dominated by the remarkable establishment bearing the name of Arthur Lasenby Liberty, whose path intersected the high road of English Taste on at least two occasions. As a young man working in the oriental warehouse of Farmer and Rogers, Liberty rose to managerial rank, by which time Dante Gabriel Rossetti had already introduced him to James McNeill Whistler as a useful connection in the hunt for 'aesthetic' artefacts. At last, having enhanced both the prestige and the profits of the firm, Liberty requested a partnership, and on being turned down, opened his own shop just across the street. Within five years Farmer and Rogers were out of business and Liberty *en route* to immortality,

which he finally clinched when W. S. Gilbert, seeking for someone to transmute his designs for 'The Mikado' into reality, asked Liberty, who kindly obliged.

By the time of this photograph Liberty's was an institution with bizarre conventions of its own. Other Regent Street shops had assistants, Liberty had cicerones. Other shop assistants said 'Good morning, madam' but a cicerone waits until he is spoken to. Other shop assistants, when asked to deliver the goods, ask for a name and address, but not your cicerone, who was expected to recognise every customer by sight and to have memorised their paralysingly fashionable multi-addresses. Hemlines went up, but not at Liberty's where the lady cicerones sported floor-

length gowns into the 1930s. The world came to Liberty's doors, including Indian princes, and several crowned heads, not all of which remained crowned long enough for the order to be fulfilled. In 1914 a Liberty cicerone was busy learning Russian in preparation for a visit to St Petersburg, where the Tsar Nicholas, having decided that the best way of alleviating the sufferings of the serfs was to order new drapes for his palace, had ordered them from Liberty's. In the same year the firm lost another order when, in mid-contract for the Archduke Franz Ferdinand, the customer was assassinated, which caused not only the Great War but also the cancellation of the contract. Everything happened to Liberty's.

6942.

A LONE BICYCLIST, harbinger of the modern age, threads a path between the carriages rattling in state along Regent Street. In later years, Londoners were to have difficulty in grasping the implications of the simple act of pedalling. A bicycle needed no stable, no oats, no livered servants to control its path. A bicycle, once acquired, required no fuel, no outlay, no license. The bicycle was the beginning of cheap private travel, and conspired with the excursion train to administer the death-blow to the chaperone.

It was the universal symbol of emancipation for the great mass of people, but it would also have been understood, at the time this photograph was taken, as an indication of something altogether more sensational.

That man pedalling down Regent Street takes quiet pride in his status; he assumes parity with the coachmen almost without thinking of it. But his sentiments are probably closer to those of the young men in *The Diary of a Nobody*, who yearn for a mention in weekly cyc-

ling magazines, than to the heroine of Rose Macaulay's *Told By an Idiot*, who defined the prosaic Raleighs and Rudges as 'the nearest approach to wings permitted to men and women here below', and who is later described in terms which would no doubt reduce our pedalling man in the cap and sober suit to bewilderment: 'She had everything. A bicycle, a husband, a baby a house, freedom, love, literary and social opportunity, charming friends. Life was indeed felicitious to such as she.'

EMBODIMENT OF THE plebeian dream, retail trade – a nice little business bringing in some ready money. In Edwardian Notting Hill, the blind are reseating chairs, the local bookshop is pushing a masterpiece called *A Haunted Hunting Lodge*, while above, the genial impresario Leo announces the expansion of his premises. Williams the ironmonger has ingeniously

blocked off his own entrance with a pendulous multiplicity of buckets and baskets. But it is that awning under whose umbrella there passes the lady in the white blouse which suggests the most alarming images. The awning advertises a corset manufactory, and the window display is at least erotic enough to have turned the head of the young blade in the knickerbockers. But

what is the awful import of those giant letters overhead? Even across the gulf of the years they seem to be snapping at the heels of posterity with sinister persistence. Corsets and teeth.

The explorer hastily moves on, to one of a succession of St James's Markets, off the Haymarket, and is immediately impressed by the multifarious nature of retail trade. That

blackboard propped up between barber and newsagent advertises the sale of coal, coke and wood, with possibly the derelict wheelbarrow representing reserve stocks. R. White and Batey are even now in the fizzy drink game, but probably the range of Mr Slade's shop with its copies of *The Morning Post* slowly dampening in the rack, embraces goods at least as wide in their application as those of Conrad's Mr Verloc, whose anarchistic pursuits were camouflaged by a welter of flyblown envelopes, comics, photographs, patent medicines and rubber stamps. The hint of a vintage opal sky seems more edifying than these last days of a squalid sidestreet. But appearances in London are usually deceptive. It was in St James's Market that a Mr Fortnum first bumped into a Mr Mason.

THE HOUSE OF WAX stands four-square to the world, having survived terrifying vicissitudes before being washed up on the high shores of Empire. In this peaceful scene no trace of the lurid past of its founder remains. The bodies have all been buried under generations of stolid insularity. And yet the young Marie Tussaud had lived through the French Revolution, shared a cell with the future Empress Josephine, modelled the head of the dead Marat and preserved the features of the Queen, saving herself from the guillotine only through her gift for making wax effigies of the heads of the less fortunate. In 1802 she wisely came to England, exhibiting in Baker Street. After her death the collection found a permanent home in Marylebone Road. The canopy at the western end will one day lead to a cinema and restaurant, both doomed. In 1940 an unknown lunatic employed by the German government will drop a bomb on the building in the belief that the best way of bringing in the brave new world is to destroy all the enemy's dummies. However, the bomb will smash only the cinema at the western end of the block, which will later be rebuilt as the Planetarium.

Despite the sedateness of the scene, Tussaud's is doing good business, and no wonder when the opposition consists of plays like 'The Wilderness'. This is an unintentionally comic piece by the actor-dramatist H. V. Esmond, in which the young hero, a noodle with £30,000 a year, gripes that 'there are no wild flowers in Bond Street', a complaint of such wonderful assininity that it tempted Max Beerbohm, when he reviewed the play in April 1901 to convict it of 'sickly fatuousness'. Madame Tussaud's exhibits were no doubt more lifelike than Mr Esmond's. The founder's son once insisted that his attendants were not encouraged to look like the dummies, to which James Bone replied that there was one commissionaire who sat so stiffly as to be almost indistinguishable from one of the figures. 'Ah', said Mr Tussaud slowly, 'I'm afraid nothing can be done with him. You see, he *is* a figure.'

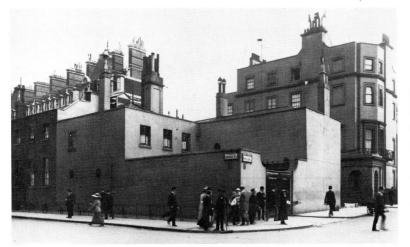

NOTHING COULD LOOK more ordered than this view of Marble Arch in 1923 (right).

Lengthening shadows point towards the West End; in the middle of the road a lone hiker carrying a stick, a package slung over his shoulder, marches on, while the policeman in the bottom right-hand corner tactfully looks the other way. It is difficult for anyone in this scene to imagine these streets echoing to the clangour of the Class War and the retail milk trade. But three years from now, when the General Strike breaks out, the road behind the Arch leading through the park will be converted into central London's milk depot, with thousands of lorries entering and leaving round the clock and the park gates guarded by police.

It is noticeable how the Arch is dwarfed by the new building behind it, Hereford House, whose eastern afterthought, round the corner in Oxford Street, houses the Marble Arch Pavilion, one of those cinematic curiosities, a cinema in the West End which nobody ever quite thinks of as a West End cinema.

The scene is modern, antiseptic, a shade grandiose, and somehow depersonalised.

In its earlier incarnation (above) this purlieus had retained those Victorian architectural proportions so reassuring to the human pygmies obliged to live under them. It is June 1914, the last lingering moment of the nineteenth century postscript. The lettering on the black door betrays the surviving presence of stables in Park Lane, which means that the street cleaner sporting the ANZAC millinery will be kept busy enough. The skyline is essentially Victorian, the hemlines almost so. What reassures the cluster of folk on the corner of Oxford Street and Park Lane is the permanence of their lives. A little trouble in Ireland perhaps, a little more from the Suffragettes and the Trade Unions, but nothing to undermine the essential steadiness of existence. Being no more psychic than their rulers, they cannot suspect that even as they enjoy the London sunshine, a Bosnian grammar schoolboy called Princip is planning the assassination of the Archduke Franz Ferdinand. In the

words of Frederick Willis: 'Nineteen hundred and fourteen is to people of my generation like a Scarlet Line drawn across the story of their lives.'

LOOKING EAST ALONG Oxford Street
in 1890, we can see that the façade
of the Princess's Theatre, over the
awning, is already blackened by
London soot, even though this is
the theatre rebuilt only two years
before. The original theatre had
been famous for the simultaneous
revival and vivisection of Shakespeare performed nightly by Charles
Kean, who was never the kind of
actor-manager to let the text get in
the way of the scenery. His cheerful

mutilations did, however, have the effect of tempting respectable London into the then still disreputable theatre, but among the purists who might not have felt that this was enough was Shakespeare himself. The briskest summary of Kean's art was achieved by G. H. Lewes, who went to see Kean as Macbeth: 'Does Charles Kean represent this character? He does not. He cannot be said to take any view of the character at all.' After Kean's day the Prin-

cess's became associated for a while with melodrama, but by the time of Charles White had been converted into a shopping centre. It was pulled down in 1931 to make way for a branch of Woolworths.

Two years earlier, further west along the street, still looking east, the sandwich boards are exhorting Victorian London to 'Run Wild at 8.30'. A milk cart clatters west out of the picture; both its modest function and the clearly second-rate

style of the shops underlines the fact that at this time Oxford Street was not thought very much of by fashionable London.

By 1908 OXFORD STREET, seen here looking east from west of the Circus, is shedding its old raffishness. The time is now past when bohemia lives in its back alleys. Fifty years before, Becky Sharp's dissolute artist-father had had a studio in Newman Street, a side-turning away in the upper left haze of this scene. In the same street the Pre-Raphaelites had sported, particularly Holman Hunt, who had here reconciled an excessive preoccupation with the ecclesiastical overtones of his paintings with a commendably unsanctified attraction for his teenaged model. Both he and the rest of the Pre-Raphaelites would have paid close attention to the greying advertisement on the Shoreditch omnibus: 'Maud Allan Matinees at the Palace Theatre'. Miss Allan (1879–1956) was a Canadian 'artistic' dancer whose 'Vision of Salome' had opened at the Palace in March to a sharp intake of Watch Committees. Years later the judge presiding over a libel case involving her Salome had rejected the performance as 'nasty', but Arnold Bennett begged to differ, saying it was merely 'poor'. To the end Miss Allan was remembered as the lady who had displayed colonial loyalty by dancing before Edward VII wearing two oyster shells and a five-franc piece.

By the 1920s London is already trapped, a horse-and-cart town struggling to accommodate the internal combustion engine. The hopeless congestion, entirely the work of White's leviathans, seems about to burst the seams of Oxford Street and overrun the department store on the left whose towers first rose in 1876. Alison Adburgham reminds us that Marshall and Snelgrove's five-story chateau houses two thousand workers, of whom seven hundred board on the premises, enjoying the facilities of library, sitting rooms, smoking rooms, committee rooms and reading rooms, and that the shop's co-founder James Marshall had, some years earlier, done a deal with the Midland Railway, which wanted to run its lines through his Mill Hill estate. Marshall allowed them to run their lines provided he had the right to stop any express train to suit his convenience.

The store's dignity was far above the garish commercial standards flying from the battlements of more modest establishments on the south side of the street. It is the banners as much as anything which endow stolid old Oxford Street with the chromatic gaiety of a Chinese New Year display. The banner is a form of advertisement whose days are numbered, but for the moment the air is alive with the whickering of flags whose proprietors are evidently willing to take a chance with the whimsicality of London breezes. Later students of the advertising banner were to notice cinemas whose billing of 'The Adventures of Sherlock Holmes' and 'Alexander's Ragtime Band' had been edited by the winds to read 'The Dentures of Shlock Les' and 'Alex's Rat Band'. The most telling fragment of evidence in this photograph to show that the world has changed is neither the motor buses, nor the School of Languages, nor even the frightful implications of 'the shingled head'. The banner in the upper right foreground sports a device which would have seemed strange indeed to denizens of the old Princess's. In those comic operetta days nobody had need to bother with passports.

ELFRIDGE'S
MENS DEPT'S
SELFRIDGE & Co Ltd
SELFRIDGE & Co Ltd
PLEASE HELP
SELFDENIAL WEEK
PLEASE HELP
LUX
DUNLOP TYRES
HEINZ 57
GENERAL
LL6821

SYMBOL OF THE NEW WORLD. In the 1890s the Wisconsin huckster Gordon Selfridge, who had raised himself by a paroxysm of buying and selling from a twelve-year-old errand boy to junior partner in Marshall Field of Chicago, came to London and was amused by the pretence of leading shopkeepers that they were administering country houses, and by the abject counter-hand subservience so finely depicted in H. G. Wells' *Kipps.* In 1906 Selfridge returned and began to build his new empire. He leased 40,000 square feet at the western, unfashionable end of Oxford Street, and, amid a trumpeting of publicity never before known in London, opened his doors, which gave on to 130 departments, including a bargain basement, reading and rest rooms, post office, roof garden, and the ice cream soda fountain at whose elysian counters the juvenile Noël Coward received maternal rewards for being cast as a mussel in *The Goldfish.*

By 1923, when these scenes were shot, Selfridge was about to absorb the entire block into his dream. He would hardly have cared to associate himself with the sentiments of the bus hoarding for the Salvation Army's Self-Denial Week; whatever his virtues, self-denial was not among them. An early poster had boasted his 'dedication to Woman's service', a claim which he believed in so fervently that he carried it into his private life, which at one point collided with that of William Somerset Maugham. In 1911 Maugham met Mrs Syrie Wellcome, currently engaged in an affair with Selfridge. Syrie soon forsook the charge account at the store which always comprised part of the favours bestowed by Selfridge on his mistresses, and married Maugham, leaving Selfridge to console himself

with Gaby Deslys, 'la grande horizontale'. His life now soared to a climax of pleasure, which included regular trips to Deauville to subsidise the local casino, and siege operations against assorted chorus girls – operations whose commencement was always signalled by the parking of his Rolls Royce outside the relevant stage door. In 1940 the banks tactfully removed him from office and pensioned him off. Posterity can get a picture of Selfridge by examining Arthur Fenwick, in Maugham's play 'Our Betters' (1915). Any lingering doubts that Fenwick was supposed to be Selfridge are dispelled by Maugham's passionate insistence that he was supposed to be someone else.

OXFORD STREET GRINDING to a halt, as usual, on arrival at the collision between Tottenham Court Road, New Oxford Street and Charing Cross Road. In later years this mess will be named St Giles's Circus, an imposing title which will change nothing. These two photographs, taken within minutes of each other during Charles White's dog-day tour of the London streets in 1923, give some idea of the hopeless disparity between the width of the road and the weight of the traffic. White knew it was pure vanity attempting to arrange timetables when the impediments included the private motorist, Harrod's delivery vans,

soap lorries, and, most deadly of all, the surviving horse and cart. There is one other obstructive element impeding the eastward-trundling London buses and that is the eastward-trundling London buses, which appear to be sabotaging each other as they come to the great divide of the Circus. The canopy on the north side announcing a Lyons teashop is a reminder that the corner site, which in five years from now will be transformed into the mock-Bavarian mountains of the Oxford Street Corner House, once rang to the music and laughter of the Oxford Music Hall. The stage door faced a public house whose

saloon bar, as Frederick Willis recalled it, 'was as quiet and peaceful as an exclusive West End club'. But then, Willis had never been inside an exclusive West End club, whose members, perhaps, were those mysterious enemies of women whose machinations were so fell that White's employers blazoned their iniquities across the sides of omnibuses.

EVEN IN THESE SIMPLE times, the pun has made inroads on the chaste world of advertising. Although fish restaurants called 'The Contented Sole' and 'Cod Almighty' are still fancies lying deep in the womb of time, Oxford Street boasts a sign saying 'This is the Plaice', erected by a restaurant proprietor whose amenities include 'Dining Room Upstairs, Popular Prices, Quick Service'. On the far side of the Circus, where one day the Dominion Theatre will be jostled by the dummies in the shop windows of Montague Burton, there are two revealing items of information. At the Prince of Wales Theatre a revue is running called 'This is London'; the eye which falls on this sensational disclosure cannot help taking in also the even more staggering news that 'insurance costs you nothing'. Between these two statements, one comically superfluous, the other idiotically dishonest, *The Daily News* boasts of being the town's brightest broadcaster. It is no surprise that its owners feel obliged to assert their sheet's identity so stridently, because these days there is always a danger that the readers will forget exactly which newspaper it is they are reading.

And yet no newspaper in history ever had birth-pangs more prestigious than *The Daily News*, which first appeared in 1846 as the brainchild of Charles Dickens. Dreaming of a Liberal daily to challenge the authority of *The Times*, and having no more than the work of ten men to do at the time, Dickens became its first editor. Seventeen issues later he resigned, handing over to his confidant, John Forster, who also resigned soon after. *The Daily News* continued to represent the Liberal interest, although by 1923, with its hoarding appearing over St Giles's Circus, there are very few people left in England who know what the Liberal interest is, thanks to the antics of Messrs Asquith and Lloyd George. Seven years after this moment, *The Daily News* will have to dispense with advertisements of this kind, because, as a consequence of swallowing up *The Daily Chronicle*, it will become *The News Chronicle*, itself destined to disappear one day after manoeuvres considered by many Fleet Street moralists to be as fishy as the fare in that first-floor restaurant.

THE AUTUMN OF 1899 (below). Charles Wyndham, with becoming modesty, has decided to name his new theatre after himself. Perhaps that hansom is waiting for Wyndham to emerge with his head whirling at the thought of all the great nights to come. Those great nights will not quite go according to plan. The playbills announce that the first production to be presented at the new theatre will be something by Henry Arthur Jones. This was not to be. For reasons which have long since disappeared into the limbo of forgotten things, Jones failed to come up with the goods, and Wyndham opened instead with an old warhorse of Tom Robertson's adapted from the French, 'David Garrick'. Although the façade of the theatre looks familiar enough to a later age, the original

Wyndham's held more people in its early years, around twelve hundred, compared to its eventual capacity of just under eight hundred. Wyndham, whose stage urbanity spurred Arnold Bennett to emulation, played a wide variety of roles and gave the same performance in all of them. Those anticipatory playbills of his also announce the coming appearance of the actress Mary Moore, a leading lady of his who had recently been promoted to the role of Mrs Wyndham. Her husband, ever a thoughtful man, and the very soul of urbanity, had pondered long over the problem of how to link his new theatre with his new wife. At last he solved the problem by gracing the proscenium arch with a bust depicting the owner's wife flanked by a pair of abject acolytes who turn out on closer examination to be Sheridan and Goldsmith.

The hoardings on the north wall facing the side of the new theatre hint at the looming century – among the items advertised is the new Standard Remington Typewriter. But still the old technology remains in evidence. A few feet south of the munching horse is a knifegrinder's cart, unattended for the moment, but at the disposal of the critics should their weapons require it when they arrive for the grand opening on November 16, 1899.

A quarter of a century later, further down Charing Cross Road on the western side, new buildings have ousted the famous jam and pickle factory of Messrs Crosse and Blackwell (above left). Jackie Coogan is presenting his unlikely collaboration with Charles Dickens, while further east that symbol of naughty decadence, the Turkish Bath, stands out against a clear grey sky.

The Imperial Hotel (right) in Russell Square, is a perfect example of Edwardian exuberance, and one of the few architectural images in White's collection which suffers from an absence of colour. Its russet bricks, profligate terra-cotta effects, green mansard roof, and what Hermione Hobhouse describes as 'the glazed and gilded sunburst on the façade', are not so much

hinted at by the processes of black-and-white photography. It was the eventual fate of the hotel to be sacrificed to the belief that cleanliness is next to Godliness. It was handed over to the demolition crews in 1966 partly through its lack of bathrooms.

THE PHOTOGRAPHS IN this book represent the view of Charles White as he surveyed the evolving streets of the world's greatest city. These streets are, so to speak, in historical midstream, with a horsedrawn past and a car-choked future. But at last so far afield did the explorers come that they reached open country, and having reached it, corrupted it instantly and utterly. No more sensational demonstration can be found than at Golders Green. In 1901 it comprised a few scattered houses sealed off from London by Hampstead Heath; when in that year a plan was proposed to provide a tram service, protesters described the area as a place 'where there are roses in the hedgerows and the larks are singing.' For the moment, rusticity triumphed; the big news in the local paper for 1902 was of horse-stealing. In 1906 the celebrated soprano Ella Russell took a Golders Green villa because 'it would be so peaceful in the country'. As for Hendon, it had no electricity, no telephones, no fire brigade.

But there were portents. Madame Russell could see from her windows the prophetic glow of the gas lamps marching along Finchley Road; a board was seen nailed to a pig shed offering building sites. In 1902 the Underground Railway was given permission to extend its line. Five years later the first electric trains racketed into the emergent suburb. On Sundays Londoners came out to relax and found the local band playing light airs for their delectation in the station forecourt. By then the villa owners had sold up and gone, leaving the world to darkness and the estate agents. From October 1909, a 'Theatre Express' left Leicester Square Station for Golders Green every night at 11.30. Theatricals saw the new bolthole as an ideal compromise between

town and country, and it is symbolic that the two most famous British female stage artists both moved out here, Marie Lloyd and Madame Pavlova, who formally opened Golders Green's first cinema, the Ionic, in 1913. By 1925 the combined population of Golders Green and Hendon was thirty thousand. The deed was done. And yet, only twenty years before, when the Atlas had run from Hendon and Golders Green to Oxford Circus, a local historian described the trip as 'the prettiest omnibus route in London'. But for how long? These two views of Golders Green – in 1904 looking north-east from the Regent's Park Road, with the site of the underground station on the right, and again in 1922, looking north from the same road – tell more graphically than any words the story of the streets of London.

Postscript

Photographs preserve the face of the past; they cannot do much about its spirit, which relies for its survival on keenness of observation allied to gifts of expression possessed by those writers who address themselves to such matters. A life lived in London requires for its full savouring an awareness of what once was, not in remote antiquity, but the day before the day before yesterday. There was once a newspaper reporter whose editorial brief was to walk the streets daily and keep walking until he encountered the theme of an essay; after nearly two hundred explorations he wrote that Londoners are like players rehearsing a play while the scene-shifters are at work, a conclusion to which he was drawn irresistibly one morning while contemplating some excavations in the city:

> How amazing to gaze down into that pit where the record of London lies clear as layers of cream in a cake: Victorian, Georgian, Stuart, Plantagenet, Norman, Anglo-Saxon, and Roman. It stops there, for there it began. Below, nothing but clay and ooze.

And it is because epochs do not terminate themselves tidily, like chapter headings in a history primer, but overlap and retrace their own steps in a variety of bewildering ways, that the Londoner soon finds that he is living, not simply in his own time, but simultaneously in his father's time, his grandfather's, and so on depending on how far back he feels inclined to delve. The evidence is scattered about him in the richest profusion if only he has eyes to see and a spirit of inquiry to gratify.

One example among many in my own life was my association, in the days of my musical apprenticeship, with a large, handsome old house on the corner of Devonshire Terrace and Marylebone Road. It was an institution familiar to the thousands of performers who underwent searching trials of ability on its premises before juries of feeble-minded entrepreneurs and middlemen. This was Dineley's Studios, a congeries of rooms, closets and garden huts, each provided with a piano and a set of music stands; a ramshackle collection of monastic cells enjoying unchallenged sway as London's most useful set of rehearsal rooms.

Time without number did I trudge along Marylebone Road to Dineley's for an assignation with destiny, there to set out my wordly artistic goods before experts hardly competent to judge. Often the clash would take place in some elegant, high-ceilinged room with only two authentic cornerpieces to the cornice, the other two having disappeared in the unrecorded past when the room was bisected in the name of commercial expediency. For me Dineley's was convenient. I was familiar with its convolutions, it was only a short walk from my home, and in some odd way it struck me as having a congenial attitude to life, almost as though it were possible, in the old Dickensian sense, for inanimate objects to possess animate characteristics.

One day the affinity explained itself, when it dawned on me that all these years I had been puffing and snorting my renditions of 'After You've Gone' and 'Stardust' in the house once occupied by Charles Dickens and his family, and that it was in these sliced-up rooms that he had written of Copperfield and Dombey, in these chambers that friends had come to dine on venison and listen to a first reading of 'American Notes', on these floorboards that the owner and his friend Mark Lemon had celebrated Twelfth Night by dancing in their shirt-sleeves, and in the large drawing-room that one night at a Christmas party Jane Welsh Carlyle reached the conclusion that, 'there was no more witty speech uttered in all the aristocratic, conventional drawing-rooms throughout London that night as among us little knot of blackguardist literary people who felt ourselves above all rules, and independent of the universe.' That house was more redolent of the man who once occupied it than any of his other London residences, a fact which counted for nothing when the time came for the speculators to profit from its destruction.

Only two groups made serious attempts to stay the execution – the Dickens Fellowship, understandably anxious to preserve a fragment of the authentic environment, and the Variety Artists Federation, equally anxious to save a considerable professional amenity. But the house went, and today its headstone is a chunk of masonry whose façade flings a derisory bone to the shades of Copperfield and company in the form of a bas-relief showing the sculpted faces of a few characters from the novels. The act of despoliation was perhaps less spectacular than the removal of the Euston Arch which soon followed it, but in terms of domestic architecture, the destruction of that house was one of the more gratuitous acts of vandalism of my years in the borough. So long as No. 1, Devonshire Terrace continued to stand, it remained possible for the twentieth century to return to the nineteenth, to retrace the steps of a genius, to savour the sights and sounds which had once animated him, and, most important of all, to understand the scale of the world through which he once moved. Once the deed was done, a link with the Victorian past had been smashed.

In the case of Dickens, there remain enough eyewitness accounts for modern man to reconstruct a picture of what London life must once have been like. For the less august and more obscure locations, those matter-of-fact street scenes scattered through the pages of this book, the researcher is heavily reliant on those writers who preserved the facts. These witnesses who sensed, perhaps without realising it at the time, that even as they wrote, the scene-shifters were at work, that dusk was creeping on and that if they were not quick with their reportage, all the evidence would be gone before morning. It is to this group of men that this book dedicates itself, because without their testimony, half the text could never have been written. That reporter who was instructed to walk the streets each day until the fluke of circumstance should provide him with a theme was H. V. Morton, whose trilogy, *The Heart of London, The Spell of London* and *The Nights of London*, provides a portrait of everyday life in the streets in the mid-1920s which, although possessing the virtues of light journalism rather than of heavy literature, remains, by its very modesty, a richly diverting and sometimes moving work for the Londoner who comes after. Morton stands off from his scenes and his people because he senses that by distancing himself from his own subject he can give himself the freedom to indulge in harmless romantic reverie. Most of his essays comprise metropolitan daydreams loosely based on the facts, unlike Frederick Willis, a hatter-turned-annalist in whose steady, sentimental prose there sounds the authentic voice of the Edwardian petty artisan revelling in the sheer

profusion of effects once to be enjoyed at little or no expense in London.

Of the other explorers of the town, Arnold Bennett and J. B. Priestley brought to the task the romantic impressionability of the provincial eye, a romanticism intensified in the casual reports of the foreigner Henry James, a soul so fastidious that he found the clatter of the hansom cabs unacceptable, a gourmet so demanding that when one afternoon in a London hotel he was temerarious enough to call for fresh fruit out of season, he was bewildered to find an ancient retainer approaching with a dish of gooseberries and currants. Compton Mackenzie was a schoolboy connoisseur of the various omnibuses plying for hire in the Kensington streets of his boyhood, and V. S. Pritchett, child of an itinerant family which settled for a while in Dulwich, developed in time the most comprehensive overview of the town achieved by any writer of his generation. C. H. Rolph's *London Particulars* is an invaluable account of growing up in Edwardian Finsbury Park and Fulham, and working in the City, while the delicious whimsical virtues of John Betjeman's *London's Historic Railway Stations* are too well-known to require any further elucidation. J. M. Barrie is usually thought of as a professional Scot, but he was, after all, one of the most famous of all the Adelphi residents and a man with an acute eye for the passing moment. Once it had passed, after the evidence had been gathered up in dustcarts and whisked away, much of the proof of what had once been there was to be found in that elegant anguished cry, *Lost London*, by Hermione Hobhouse, and in that comprehensive architectural disquisition, *London 1900* by Alastair Service.

There remain two chroniclers of the London streets, two consummate artists without whose legacy it would be impossible to attempt the compilation of a volume of this kind. There is H. M. Tomlinson, the prosodist of Dockland, a writer who has grasped more completely than any I know the mystic relationship between the Londoner and his city, or, more to the point, between the villager and his village. Tomlinson, a native of Poplar, once observed, without the slightest show of theatricality, 'Cut the kind of life you find in Poplar, and I must bleed. I cannot detach myself, and write of it. Like any other atom, I would show the local dirt, if examined.' Tomlinson was the first London specialist to demonstrate to me that London was a subject at all, and although his actual words appear only very sparingly in this book, the spirit of his attitude pervades every caption. So too does that of James Bone, one-time London editor of *The Manchester Guardian*, an investigator with a taste for the transient, the doomed, the obsolescent. Time and again Bone reported some social event insignificant in itself but possessing an overpowering symbolic impact. His descriptions of the demolition of the Adelphi, the last night of the old Savage Club, the passing of the Gaiety Theatre, of Gatti's Music Hall, of Morley's Hotel, are rich in those odd little details which can, more than statistics, more even than photographs, illuminate a past which is at once only just around the corner and yet as remote as the Ptolemys. I regret the absence of Covent Garden from this collection of London scenes, because its inclusion would have given me the excuse to include Bone's description of the old Tavistock Hotel, and:

> that old Crown Colony gentleman who had been there thirty seven years, and, particularly, what became of his thousand collars, which he is said to have amassed in his cathedral-like bedroom during that period? He never destroyed or gave away a collar, but when he was tired of it, or displeased with it, he placed it in a corner of his bedroom, not to be disturbed. And so the mass grew, and it became a sort of article of pride with him, and no one was allowed to touch the low-toned pyramid.

On the other hand, several of the photographs do stray on to Bone's territory, and of all the facts and reflections I discovered in my researches, none seemed more delightful to me, or seemed to pierce the mystery of the past with a beam more illuminating, than Bone's solemn recording of the fact that Anderton's Hotel in Fleet Street was the last establishment of its kind in London to provide carpet slippers for its clientele.

Finally, there are two novelists who, although Kentish born, are, in a literary sense, representative Londoners. Many of H. G. Wells's hapless young men wandered the very streets depicted in this book, and it was their experiences which time and time again sprung to mind whenever I peered into the older photographs. Perhaps Wells was the second-best London reporter of all; certainly there is no need to name the best. One of the greatest travel books in the language is *Sketches by Boz*, a work which tells more of vital import about the streets of London than any other three books I know. Were the records of the London of one hundred and fifty years ago to be destroyed, it would be possible to deduce most of them from the complete works of Dickens. But that world lingered on with astonishing tenacity; some of the vistas of the 1880s are unchanged from those of the Dickensian heyday; the main streets of the 1920s might have seemed grossly unfamiliar to him, but had he strayed down the side alleys into the courts of the working class, he would have known his bearings instantaneously. Today, almost all the London preserved in this book has disappeared. The most mundane scenes have acquired the patina of romance simply by being lost forever. In the words of L. P. Hartley, 'the past is a foreign country; they do things differently there.'

Index